DEALING WITH
DIFFICULT PARENTS

Communicating with parents is one of the most challenging and potentially stressful tasks that teachers face daily. Whether trying to resolve a heated argument or delivering bad news, it is essential to know how to handle difficult situations and establish positive relationships with your students' parents. In this updated second edition of the bestselling book *Dealing with Difficult Parents*, award-winning educators Todd Whitaker and Douglas J. Fiore help you develop a repertoire of tools and skills for comfortable and effective interaction with parents.

The book's features include:

- Tools to help you understand parents' motivations and how to work with them rather than against them;
- Detailed scripts for dealing with even the most stubborn and volatile parents;
- New strategies for increasing parent involvement to foster student success;
- An all-new chapter on the role that social media can play in interacting with parents; and
- A new chapter on initiating contact with parents to build positive credibility.

This must-read book will equip you with the skills you need to expertly navigate even the most challenging encounters with parents, and walk away feeling that you have made a positive and meaningful impact.

DEALING WITH DIFFICULT PARENTS
SECOND EDITION

Todd Whitaker and Douglas J. Fiore

Routledge
Taylor & Francis Group

NEW YORK AND LONDON

Second edition published 2016
by Routledge
711 Third Avenue, New York, NY 10017

and by Routledge
2 Park Square, Milton Park, Abingdon, Oxon, OX14 4RN

Routledge is an imprint of the Taylor & Francis Group, an informa business

First edition published by Routledge, 2001

Library of Congress Cataloging-in-Publication Data
Whitaker, Todd, 1959–
    Dealing with difficult parents / by Todd Whitaker and Douglas J. Fiore. —
Second edition.
        pages cm
    Includes bibliographical references.
    1. Parent-teacher relationships—United States.   2. Home and school—
United States.   3. Interpersonal conflict.   4. Conflict management.   I. Fiore,
Douglas J., 1966–   II. Title.
    LC226.6.W55 2016
    371.19′2—dc23
    2015023522

ISBN: 978-1-138-93867-0 (pbk)
ISBN: 978-1-315-67555-8 (ebk)

Typeset in Palatino
by Apex CoVantage, LLC

Contents

About the Authors

Dr. Todd Whitaker is a professor of education leadership at Indiana State University in Terre Haute, Indiana. Prior to coming to Indiana, he coached and taught at the middle and high school levels in Missouri. Following his teaching experience, he served as a middle school, junior, and high school principal. In addition, Dr. Whitaker served as middle school coordinator for new middle schools.

Dr. Whitaker has been published in the areas of principal effectiveness, teacher leadership, change, and staff motivation. He has written 40 books including *What Great Teachers Do Differently, Dealing with Difficult Teachers, Motivating & Inspiring Teachers* and *What Connected Educators Do Differently*. He is a highly sought after speaker for educators.

Todd is married to Beth, a former teacher and principal, who serves as director of the Faculty Center for Teaching Excellence at Indiana State. Beth and Todd have three children, Katherine, Madeline, and Harrison.

Dr. Douglas J. Fiore is currently the interim provost at Ashland University in Ashland, Ohio. Prior to coming to Ohio, he served in faculty and leadership roles at Virginia State University, Virginia Commonwealth University, and the University of West Georgia. Dr. Fiore began his educational career teaching at the elementary school level in Indiana. Following his teaching experience, he served as an elementary school principal in two Indiana schools.

Dr. Fiore has been published in the areas of school–community relations, leadership theory, principal effectiveness, and school culture and has presented at numerous national and state conferences. He is the author of eight books including the best-selling textbook, *School-Community Relations*, as well as *Introduction to Educational Administration: Standards, Theories and Practice*, and *Six Types of Teachers: Recruiting, Retaining and Mentoring the Best*.

Doug is the proud father of three daughters, Meagan, Amy, and Katherine.

Preface

One of the most challenging and potentially unnerving tasks that we as educators deal with on a regular basis is interacting with parents. This may not be true of all parents, or maybe even most parents, but there is always that parent who is a special challenge. The parent who is bossy, volatile, argumentative, aggressive, or maybe the worst—apathetic—can even make us question our abilities and ourselves. As educators, we are often taken aback the first time we deal with a hostile parent. We might be uncomfortable, intimidated, or just caught off guard. However, if we do not figure out effective and appropriate ways to interact with these parents, we may become apprehensive about communicating with other parents. Eventually, this may lead to a general discomfort or fear any time we have contact with parents.

Being able to successfully interact in these situations is essential. Developing phrases to use, being able to control the dialogue, and being sensitive to trigger words to avoid are skills that are learned through experience. However, it is valuable to have specific language that is appropriate for multiple situations that allows us to accomplish our needs—and hopefully even allows us to develop a more positive relationship with these parents for the future.

Another tough situation that all educators face is delivering bad news to good parents. Being able to do this effectively and in an appropriate manner is critical to developing needed support from parents. This is true whether telling parents about a discipline situation, recommending placement in a special needs program, or informing them about a child's struggles with grades. Establishing and expanding a repertoire of tools is a critical need for everyone in education.

This book will help teachers, principals, superintendents and all educators increase their skills in working with the most challenging parents you come in contact with. Additionally, educators can learn and develop specific strategies to help deliver less than positive news in an appropriate manner to all of our constituents.

We will also provide tools that can help you build credibility with all parents. This can increase the level of trust and support that is imperative in building the needed parent–school relationship, which will allow greater success for all students. Initiating positive contact with parents is essential in this process. For all educators, if we do not initiate positive contact with parents, then the only contact we may have is negative. When we get into this pattern, then we become very hesitant to inform or even interact with the adults in our students' lives. Being able to comfortably and effectively make educator-initiated contact with parents is a skill that all of us must learn and practice.

Many of the situations we face are challenging. This book will provide you with specific language, understanding, and resources that you can immediately use in interacting with every parent in your community.

Introduction to the Second Edition

This is one of those books you hope you do not have to write a new edition to. We hoped that eventually parents' skill levels would improve and they would realize how generally educators truly are on their side. However, at times, the opposite seems to be true. Home situations continually seem to deteriorate and poverty levels seem to increase annually. Other schools have issue with overbearing or 'helicopter' parents who hover over their kids or their kids' schools to an inappropriate level. How can teachers best deal with all of the challenges they face when interacting with parents, families, and the loved ones of the students they have in their classrooms?

Additionally, social media has brought about more opportunities to interact with parents and possibly more expectations that we do so. How can we balance these demands with increasing pressure from testing, standards, and legislative mandates?

Teachers and administrators have given us much praise about the specific strategies in the first edition of *Dealing with Difficult Parents*. They loved the word-for-word language they were provided that enabled them to deal effectively with the most challenging or volatile parents. This edition is updated to give educators an even deeper understanding of the parents they interact with and the homes where their students come from. There are also numerous additional tips on working with parents, as well as specific scripts to help teachers know precisely what to say and how to say it when they face the most challenging situations with parents. We've added an entire chapter on the best way to initiate contact with all parents so you can get them off of your back and onto your side, and we infused new ideas into every chapter.

Good luck in this most challenging area. We are confident that this edition will help you refine your skills and increase your abilities to deal with the most difficult parents . . . and with those who are not so difficult, too!

1

Dealing with Difficult Parents

An Overview

There are many tasks that we educators have to deal with, but there may not be any that send shivers down our spines as much as dealing with a difficult parent. Being yelled at, intimidated, threatened, or just flat-out being treated rudely are things that teachers, principals, superintendents, and everyone in education dreads having to face. And in some ways, the possibility that these things will happen, and our ability to get ourselves worked up that these things might happen, all add to the burden that we face because of difficult parents.

Additionally, having to deliver bad news to good and positive parents is no fun. Is there some way that we can do these things more effectively? Are there specific techniques and approaches that we can utilize and rely on during our most heated situations? That is the purpose of this book.

In Part I, we attempt to help you understand why parents are the way they are. Although there may be different influences and circumstances today, we also explore similarities between today's parents and those of previous generations. In Part II, we provide tools to help you refine your parent interaction skills so you can become more effective in communicating with all parents. You may already be using some of these tools, but hopefully there will be many that you can add to your bag of tricks.

Parts III and IV provide specific language to help you deal effectively with the most troubling scenarios. Dialogue is provided to help you deal with the most difficult parents and work effectively with parents in the most challenging of situations. "What if the parent is right?," "The power of the apology," "Delivering bad news," and "Dealing with the 'F' word—Fair" are just a few of the situations that are described in specific detail. We examine the power of car sales clerks and learn how to use their persuasive approaches to our advantage in working with the families of our students.

We also provide a section on increasing parent involvement. Traditionally, we think of involved parents as those who join the PTA or volunteer to make cookies. Both of those things are important, but how children can most benefit is by their parents being involved at home. We take a dual focus by centering on parent involvement at school and parent involvement with their children at home.

The Importance of Parents

There are a couple of items that we need to clarify in this book. The first is that when we use the word *parent*, we are being very inclusive. Rather than repeatedly saying parent/guardian or parent/grandparent or parent/adult, we rely on using the simplest approach possible—parent. We are also very sensitive to the fact that when we send home mass mailings, back-to-school night invitations, or information about an upcoming field trip, we need to be very careful with the specific way we word the salutation. We cannot flippantly use the word parent when the information is being addressed to the many different family makeups in which our students reside.

However, we also do not apologize for using that term in this book. It reminds me of how I use the word *teacher* when I address cooks, custodians, secretaries, bus drivers, and the like, when doing speaking engagements around the country. I always explain that if children and students see us working, then we are teachers. One way or the other, if they can observe our behavior, then we are teachers. After all, if we do not model what we teach, then we are teaching something else. Similarly, the use of the word parent is for the ease of the readers, who can use the appropriate terms in their contacts with the families of their students.

What's the Deal with Today's Parents?

The other bias that we want to share at this point is that we feel that parents are parents, and they are not really that much different than they have ever been. Parents still want what is best for their children. Now, just as 50 years ago, there will always be some parents who have no idea what is best for their children or how to provide it, but they still want it. As a matter of fact, the parents we struggle with the most now are probably the grandchildren of the parents that were most challenging 50 years ago!

If we look at any point in history, there have always been belligerent and uncooperative parents. And realistically, those parents have always been the ones that we spend the most time dealing with, mainly because they often have the most uncooperative and challenging children. We do believe, though, that while people are still people and parents are still parents, many environmental factors have changed dramatically. The number of single-parent homes, mothers working full time, and broken homes of all types, have all been factors that have impacted families and therefore schools. We discuss these influences at length in the next two chapters. We also believe, though, that as adults we have to accept responsibility for our own behavior. If being a single parent was the cause of delinquent children, then every child from a single-parent home would be a delinquent, and we know this is not true at all. Additionally, regardless of societal influences, there is still no excuse for parents being rude or disrespectful to the professionals who are working with their children.

Yet, regardless of the cause and effect, the impact that some problem parents have on educators is not in dispute, and it is something that we must work with on a regular basis. In a school where I was principal, the faculty and staff used to have a belief about the role of parents and their impact on the way their children turn out. We particularly liked to use this in the spring of the year when we were worn out and had less than ideal patience toward some of our students. When things seemed most challenging in working with a particular student or students, we would remind ourselves of this: If you have any students that you just cannot tolerate any more, you feel like your patience bucket has run out, you can barely stand the thought of them walking into your classrooms tomorrow, there is one thing that you can do. There is one simple thing you can do that will give you a whole new perspective on that child, and that is—meet their parents.

It is amazing, but once we meet their parents and become aware of their family situation, our view of the student often changes dramatically. All of a sudden, we think, "That child turned out pretty good. I thought he/she was the problem of the family, but instead it looks like he/she is probably the golden child."

This sort of became a mantra for us late in the year when we were tired and our tolerance levels were not nearly as great as they needed to be for us to be effective. We would think, "I can hardly stand thinking about Billy Edwards coming in the class anymore. I guess I'd better have a conference with his parents. After that, instead of dreading him, my empathy toward him will be greatly improved. Instead of resenting him, I'll wish I could take him home."

This view was so helpful for us. And you need to know, we do not believe in ever generalizing in a negative manner regarding parents. As a matter of fact, we think understanding them is a critical part of our philosophy and a foundation of this book.

We Are Doing the Best We Know How

It is essential to understand that around 90-plus percent of parents do a pretty good job raising their children. If we think about our schools, usually only about 5 percent of the students are a real struggle. Though all students have strengths and potential areas of growth, for the most part, parents do a pretty darn good job. However, 100 percent of parents do the best they know how. We have to understand that many of their role models did not provide them the examples and structures they need to be effective parents. Oftentimes, we compare our most troubling parents' reactions to the way our own parents would have reacted or the way the other parents in our neighborhood would have reacted. And to be truthful, if you have a positive family structure, many parents do react in that exact same manner today. However, this book is about the most difficult and challenging parents that we work with and the most perplexing situations. We have already figured out how to deal with the easy ones; anybody can do that. What takes so much of our time, worry, and energy, is the 5 percent of the parents that we often have to deal with the most. It is important to keep a positive perspective regarding the students we work with and equally important to keep that productive focus when we think of and work with their parents. After all, they are the best parents that our students have.

Also, consistently remind yourself that we need to maintain a positive focus. One of the struggles we face is when we have back-to-school night or parent-teacher conferences and the turnout is less than we had hoped for. Regardless, we should realize that the people who do attend are our most important people, and we should not give in to the temptation to let the lack of attendance ruin our night for those who showed up. If only 10 percent of the parents are there, then make sure those 10 percent feel so special that they will not only come back in the future, but they will even spread the positive word to others.

Though we have to work with some less than pleasant individuals at times, we need to focus and make sure that we do not give them the power to ruin things for the people who do show up. In this book, we provide several specific ideas for increasing the turnout at these types of events, but we also need to remember that the most important people are always the ones who are there and we have to make them feel valued.

Dealing with Yourself

Dealing with difficult parents first requires that you deal with yourself. There are few absolutes in education. Generally, every rule has an exception and no matter how consistent we attempt to be, there are times when we have to vary from our plan. However, there are a few things that we need to be resolute about. Those things involve our own actions and approach.

The best advice I ever received was, "You do not have to prove who is in charge; everybody knows who is in charge." This is so true in schools. Think about the best teachers in your school (besides yourself, that is). How often do they have to prove "who is in charge" in their classroom? Almost never. Now, think about the least effective classroom managers in your school. How often do they try to prove who is in charge? Most likely, several times every hour! As a result, there are 25 students in each of their classrooms trying to prove them wrong. This same idea applies in working with challenging parents.

We never argue, yell, use sarcasm, or behave unprofessionally. The key word to focus on in that sentence is *never*. Understand that there are several reasons why we never behave in these ways. One of them is that in every situation there needs to be at least one adult and the only person you can rely on is you. Also, one of our beliefs is you never argue with difficult people. Not only because you cannot win, which is true, but also because they have a lot more practice arguing than you do. Don't they spend a great deal of time in arguments in every aspect of their life? The people we are most likely to get in an argument with probably just spent 20 minutes arguing with the checkout clerk at the grocery store. They argue at home, are confrontational at work, and probably have a great number of interactions of this manner on a regular basis.

Another reason is a core belief of ours. We never argue with an idiot. The primary reason is because anybody watching will think that there is at least one idiot arguing. And we do not have faith that they can tell which one of us the idiot really is.

Realize that we control how many arguments we get in. We also determine how often we yell or the frequency with which we use sarcasm. There is another, maybe more critical, reason we do not ever use these behaviors, and it is a much more important reason. A basic philosophy we have in the classroom is to never yell at students. Part of this is because it is not how we should ever treat anyone, much less the young people we work with. However, a second reason is that the students we are most tempted to yell at have probably been treated like that for much of their lives. We need to teach them a new way to interact, not just polish their inappropriate skills.

The same thing applies to parents. If we believe they are doing the best they know how, then one of our missions should be to help them to improve. We believe we have a responsibility as educators to consistently model appropriate behaviors for everyone that we come in contact with. And our personal view is that it needs to be 100 percent of the time. That is, we need to do it 10 days out of 10, not just nine out of 10. If you question this, then just ask yourself two questions. "How many days out of 10 do I expect the students in my classroom and school to behave themselves?" and "How many days out of 10 do I hope that parents treat me with respect and dignity?" If the answer to these questions is 10 days out of 10, then we must ensure that we behave professionally in an equal number of days ourselves.

Though we sprinkle this book with reminders of behaving in a sincere and professional manner, please keep in mind how essential it is that we always maintain that high level of respect in our actions toward the parents that we work with. If we do not, then we are most likely creating even more problems and turmoil for ourselves.

An example would be if we ever responded to a parent who is rude to us on the phone by hanging up on them. Though the original focus of the conversation may have been on the improper behavior of their son or daughter, once they complain about us hanging up on them, the focus often shifts to our own improper behavior. We want to make sure that we do not add fuel to the fire by ever behaving in an inappropriate manner.

But I Don't Want to Go to the Dentist!

Very few people race to the dentist and hope they have some significant work that needs to be done. By the same token, few among us want to deal with difficult parents. Please keep in mind that nobody wants to work with your most challenging families. This is especially true of those that are rude and offensive in the way they treat you. Please be aware that the most effective educators do not want to deal with these offensive people either. They just do. There is not a difference in desire between more and less effective educators; there is a difference in action.

That is why we focus an entire chapter on positive communication with parents. Making that first contact positive can go a long way in establishing the relations we want and building the credibility we hope to achieve. But the other reason we promote positive contact so much is that if we do not initiate positive contact with parents, then often the majority of the contact will be negative. Not only do the positive efforts on our part help build a bond between school and home, but they can also help build our own confidence in working with parents.

We are very excited about this book and hope that you find many tools that will be useful to you as you work with the parents and families of the young people that you have been entrusted with.

Part I

Today's Parents

2

Who Are These Guys?

Describing Today's Parents

Everybody is concerned with making our schools the best they can possibly be. We all want high-quality education for our children, and we collectively concern ourselves with any and all issues related to school improvement. Because of this, the many variables that affect school improvement all matter, and we all must strive to understand and manipulate these variables somewhat for our children's advantage. Highly important among these variables are parents. The involvement of parents in the education of their children is of unquestionable significance. Studies consistently indicate that student achievement increases as parents become more involved in their children's education (Hill & Craft, 2003; Gonzalez-DeHass, Willems, & Holbein, 2005). Therefore, it would seem that caring, committed educators would do everything within their control to increase parent involvement in schools, thereby enriching the total school experience for the children they serve. After all, who among us would intentionally fail to do what is in the best interests of the students in our schools?

> *The involvement of parents in the education of their children is of unquestionable significance. Studies consistently indicate that student achievement increases as parents become more involved in their children's education.*

However, there is something that is not significantly addressed in all the studies touting the benefits of parent involvement. Simply stated, some parents are just plain difficult to deal with. Some live and/or work in very challenging situations, sometimes causing them to appear and act difficult. When we consider that the most committed educators are juggling full plates, it is easy to understand why many of them feel that dealing with these difficult parents is often an insurmountable task. It *can* be, unless educators take the time to understand difficult parents and some of the difficult situations they find themselves in. Perhaps through better understanding of these difficulties, educators will feel more empowered to welcome and involve parents in the education of their students.

Depending on a variety of factors (i.e., your position in a school, the demographics of your community, the most recent dealing you had with a parent), your personal, generalized description of today's parents may or may not be a positive one. All of us, at some point in our careers, are faced with difficult parents who can single-handedly damage our faith in the institution of parenthood. In difficult and stressful times, even the most positive among us can succumb to feelings of extreme negativity brought on by dealing with these parents. Upon reflection, though, it is important to recognize that these difficult individuals are not necessarily representative of all parents. Moreover, we must remember that most parents are not intentionally difficult. In fact, our guess is that when you hear the term "difficult parents" there are only a small percentage of parents that pop into your mind.

Regardless of how you personally describe the parents you deal with in your school setting, it is important for all of us to recognize that parents today are facing different circumstances than the parents who raised us did. Please note that there is no judgment implied in the word different. It does not mean better, and it does not mean worse. It simply means different.

> *It is important for all of us to recognize that parents today are facing different circumstances than the parents who raised us did.*

As such, the purpose of this chapter is not to judge parents in relation to their involvement in their children's education, but to identify ways in which they are different from those of previous generations. This knowledge will lead us to a better understanding of how to deal effectively with parents for the benefit of all children.

Outlined ahead are several of the ways in which contemporary parents and the families they lead are different from what many of us are accustomed to. The information contained is not exhaustive, nor is it descriptive of all parents. It is however, food for thought as we learn to understand difficult parents and how to deal with them effectively. The best way to use this information is to think about it in the context of your own particular school experiences. As you read, you may find yourself conjuring up images of parents that you have worked with. This is good, for it will assist you in making the information come alive. You will understand parents best, after all, by analyzing your own experiences.

Finally, it's important to understand that none of what follows in this chapter is meant to excuse inappropriate behavior from parents. There is no excuse for parents who behave inappropriately with teachers. This information merely serves to inform us of the challenges many parents face.

Family Configurations

Research is replete with statistical information regarding the changes in family dynamics that our culture has experienced. Not only are there plenty of statistics to verify the changes, but our daily observations confirm them regularly. Among the factors receiving a great deal of attention in both statistics and observations is the working mother. This is one factor that makes today's parents different from those of previous generations. More and more, we see mothers of school-aged children pursuing careers or seeking full-time employment, often out of economic necessity. Consider that in 1940 fewer than 9 percent of all women with children worked outside the home (U.S. Bureau of Labor Statistics, 1987). In 2009, the U.S. Bureau of Labor Statistics reported that 78.9 percent of women with children between the ages of 6 and 17 were in the labor force (National Data Book, 2012).

This dramatic increase in the number of working mothers can be attributed to many causes, including inflation, the increased cost of child rearing, and the decreased likelihood of living the "American Dream" on a single income (Rank, Hirschl, & Foster, 2014). Also contributing to this increase are the substantial rise in the U.S. divorce rate and the growing percentage of women giving birth out of wedlock. As evidence, in 2014, 41 percent of American babies were born to single mothers. This represents a dramatic shift in family configurations. In fact, while widowhood was once the primary cause of one-parent families, recent statistics indicate that 50 percent of single-parent homes result from separation or divorce, and 49 percent are the consequence of children born to mothers who've never been married (U.S. Census Bureau, 2012). As we know from our observations, a very high percentage of these one-parent families are configured with the mother living with and giving primary care to the children. It is worth noting that in many cases, the term primary care is misleading. The term implies that there is somebody else giving secondary care. Yet often, many of us are finding that there is only one parent giving any care to the children. More often than not, it is the mother. In fact, of the 75 million children under the age of 18 living in U.S. households in 2014, 24.3 percent, or 18.1 million were living with their mother only; 54 percent of those children were under the age of 9.

This apparent depreciation of fatherhood creates real problems for our schools and society. Just ask any teacher what he/she thinks the effect of fatherless homes is on students. As our experience has shown, most teachers will have strong feelings on this subject. In fact, children from fatherless homes have been found to be both less productive in school and responsible for a high percentage of criminal behavior (Blankenhorn, 1995). In a study examining paternal involvement over the first 10 years of children's lives, researchers found that father-child contact was associated with better socio-emotional and academic functioning. The results indicated that children with more involved fathers experienced fewer behavioral problems and scored higher on reading achievement (Howard, Burke Lefever, Borkowski, & Whitman, 2006).

Across the U.S., nearly 7.8 million children are living in homes with grandparents present, 4.9 million live in grandparent-headed households and 2.6 million live in homes where the grandparents are the primary caregivers. Approximately 1 million children living with a grandparent do not have either parent in the house at all. All educators know that these grandparents, deserving of our highest esteem for the efforts they put in to rearing the children of their children, are often more tired and in poorer health than many of them would like to be. These issues absolutely show up in our schools.

Family Wealth

In addition to the changes family configurations have undergone, the relative wealth of American households has also experienced negative change recently. For example, in 2013, real median household income was 8 percent lower than in 2007, the year before the most recent recession. Relating this to family configurations, married-couple households had the highest median income in 2013 ($76,509), followed by households maintained by men with no wife present ($50,625). Those maintained by women with no husband present had the lowest income ($35,154). Finally, in 2013, children represented 23.5 percent of the total population and 32.3 percent of people in poverty. While it is true that many families lived in poverty during other times, such as the Great Depression, the gap between the rich and the poor and the integration of the two groups within our schools and society are considered by many to be more significant today.

Another issue related to family wealth involves the high number of homeless children in this country. Children, in fact, are by most accounts among the fastest growing segments of the homeless population. Families with children constitute approximately 35 percent of people who become homeless, with children under the age of 18 accounting for a full 25 percent of the U.S. homeless population. Additionally, 45 percent of homeless children and youth (K–12) were not attending school on a regular basis during their homelessness.

The combination of the high cost of living, low-wage jobs, and high unemployment rates only exacerbate these problems and force countless Americans to choose between food, housing, and other expenses. Studies show that money devoted to food is typically the first to be sacrificed. Families will often pay their fixed payments first, such as rent and utilities, rather than pay for food. Throughout the U.S., federal spending on housing assistance programs targeted at low-income populations is less than 50 percent of 1976 spending levels.

Family Stress

A family's configuration and lack of wealth can cause them a great deal of stress. With so many parents working longer hours and being less wealthy on a relative basis than their parents reportedly were, it is no wonder that some feel that finding 15 minutes of quality time with their children is impossible. This is particularly so as schools continue to stress parent involvement during the school day, seeming to ignore the hours parents are spending at work. The result is an ever-growing percentage of parents who feel guilty that they can't be involved in their children's education. These feelings of guilt, which may be accompanied by already existing negative feelings about school (which we'll elaborate on later in this book), lead many parents to become even less supportive than they would have been if our school personnel had shown some signs of understanding their life challenges.

There are, as we know, many reasons why families are under stress. Many of them center on issues previously discussed. In addition to the financial and structural issues, though, there is increased evidence that the adults in this country are struggling with an increase in stress-induced illnesses. This is evident when we simply look at the sharp increase in the percentage of American adults who are taking prescription drugs to deal with anxiety and other social issues.

While the previous paragraphs do not describe all of the parents that walk through the doorways of our schools, they are descriptive of an ever-growing segment of our population. School personnel need to be aware of these statistics to avoid continuing to filter our images of the world through the lenses of our own experiences. We can no longer afford to judge parents solely on the basis of how involved they appear to be in their children's education. Likewise, we cannot blindly accept

We can no longer afford to judge parents solely on the basis of how involved they appear to be in their children's education.

the lack of involvement; we know that parents play a critical role in the education of their children. Moreover, we cannot delight in the absence of our more difficult parents. Though this is often a natural reaction, as working with these difficult parents can be very annoying and time-consuming, the absence of even our most difficult parents means that we lose some valuable resource help. This is simply not fair to our students. What is needed is an understanding of today's parents, a realization that many of them do not feel that they possess the resources to be actively involved in their children's education, a commitment to increase their involvement, and strategies for dealing with them when they seem to be so difficult.

What is needed is an understanding of today's parents, a realization that many of them do not feel that they possess the resources to be actively involved in their children's education, a commitment to increase their involvement, and strategies for dealing with them when they seem to be so difficult.

Typical Behaviors of Some of Our Parents

Thinking back to some of the difficult situations that we have been involved in with parents is not a pleasant form of relaxation. Often the experience is reminiscent of nails on a chalkboard. Nevertheless, by reminding ourselves of some of these situations, we can begin to see patterns that can be helpful when we find ourselves in similar situations in the future. Our goal, in recognition of the many benefits associated with schools having positive relationships with parents, ought to be to learn from these situations. By understanding how to effectively deal with parents, particularly those living through many of the difficulties previously described, we can turn negative situations into very positive ones.

We can certainly come up with many examples of difficult parents and difficult situations from our own experiences as teachers and administrators. In fact, the odds are very good that you will be able to relate some of your own experiences with those that follow:

One example is the parent who marches into the teacher's classroom complaining that the teacher does not recognize his/her child's innate abilities. Regardless of the grade levels served by your school, it can be said with relative certainty that all of you can relate to this experience. In this particular instance, let's say that we are speaking about a kindergarten student. The parent, and it can be either mom or dad, is convinced that the child is gifted. The issue that the parent finds so upsetting is that the teacher has stated that the child does not know his/her address. The parent, obviously enraged by this, comes to see the teacher insisting that something be done about the teacher's assessment. In fact, this parent insists, this particular child has been reciting his/her home address for a full eight months!

Consider a second example. Again, though virtually any grade level could be substituted into the following situation, let's say that we are dealing with a student in the 11th grade. This particular student has gotten into a fight during a passing period between classes. In this fight, he/she threw several punches, caused injury to another student, spoke disrespectfully to a teacher, and brought chaos to an otherwise normal part of the school day. As punishment for this fight, the teacher, with support from the principal, has issued a one-day suspension from school activities. The parent, again either mom or dad will do, comes in to school to see both the teacher and the principal. The only apparent purpose for this meeting is to find out what punishment the other student who was involved in the altercation received. Despite the teacher's best efforts to keep the conversation focused on the appropriate issues, the parent does not relent and continues to demand an explanation of the other child's punishment.

Though these issues are not going to single-handedly drive too many teachers into early retirement, they do typify some of the time-consuming parent issues that educators are increasingly dealing with. The issues are not confined to the classroom, as they may have been years ago. Instead, custodians, bus drivers, counselors, classroom assistants, and other school employees are facing them as well. Without having techniques for dealing with these situations, some people may find professional work in schools to be less and less appealing. Without some sense of why parents behave like this, any effort to understand how to resolve these issues seems fruitless. However, as many of us realize, there are reasons why some parents behave similarly to those in the previous examples. Several of these reasons will be explored in subsequent chapters. Remember that parents, in many ways, are different than any of us think they ought to be. Given their circumstances, however, they are not necessarily wrong. But since they are different, dealing with them, in many cases, requires understandings and strategies that are different than what we might otherwise expect. As this book will clearly illustrate, there are specific behaviors, strategies, and techniques that will make it so much easier to deal with seemingly difficult parents and with the difficult situations you find yourself in. The first step is to understand parents. It is only after we make an honest effort to understand parents that we can really hope to employ practices to effectively deal with them.

> *Remember that parents, in many ways, are different than any of us think they ought to be. Given their circumstances, however, they are not necessarily wrong.*

> *It is only after we make an honest effort to understand parents that we can really hope to employ practices to effectively deal with them.*

Remember, parental involvement is a key to many of our best schools. It is, many believe, a significant variable in student success. So teachers—and for our purposes, all school personnel are considered teachers—must recognize and then manipulate this important variable. As leaders for all children, they must do all they can to understand and subsequently embrace our most difficult parents. Their involvement, too, will be a key in improving our schools.

As you read the remainder of this book, you will discover examples that sound much like some of those that you have lived through in your own school. You will read practical solutions that are not difficult to emulate and really work. Finally, you will come to understand the value of dealing effectively with difficult parents in a way that will make your job as a committed teacher that much more appealing.

3

What's Wrong with These Parents Anyway?

Knowing about today's parents and the situations they face assists us in understanding what typical family life is like and how different it is than family life may have been when we were growing up. This is important only to the extent that it affirms the differences teachers always have been suspecting. It does little, however, in terms of explaining just what's wrong with these parents anyway. It fails, in many ways, to explain why parents behave as they do. Examining the information available to parents today and what this information says about our educational systems is of real value in our understanding of why so many parents may view our schools with negative feelings. In addition, an understanding of the experiences that today's parents had when they were schoolchildren, themselves, sheds light on the seemingly dark reactions some of them may have toward our schools.

Perception Is Reality

Browse your favorite bookstore and you'll find many books whose titles are designed to either assist parents in holding their children's schools accountable or inform them of the problems, real or imagined, in our schools. Recent titles that have been purchased by many of our schools' parents include: *Holding*

Schools Accountable: A Handbook for Parents (Sloan, 2008), *How Parents Can Save America's Failing Schools* (Pierce, 2002), *The Good School: How Smart Parents Get Their Kids the Education They Deserve* (Tyre, 2011), *Public Schools, Public Menace: How Public Schools Lie to Parents and Betray our Children* (Turtel, 2005), and *Smart Parents, Successful Kids: How to Get What Your Child Needs (And Deserves) from Your Local School* (Tingley, 2015). A quick glance at these titles would lead one to believe that parents have at their disposal a plethora of information condemning our schools. In fact, in light of these titles, it's amazing that we don't have even more difficult parents.

In fairness to the above-mentioned authors, the condemnation of our schools may not have been their goal while writing these books. In fact, in defense of some of them, we can say with certainty that it was not their goal. However, a mere reading of these book titles clearly suggests that there is something seriously wrong with the schools our children are attending. Furthermore, there is an implication that parents can and must do something about it. With this in mind, what kind of message are parents receiving when they look at these titles on books available today? Are they receiving a message touting the quality of our work and applauding our efforts? Obviously not. If you have had the uncomfortable experience of having a parent share one of these books with you, you will understand this even better.

Now, consider this. If parents, already dissatisfied with the way in which they perceive your school to be dealing with their child, encounters books like those mentioned above, then one can bet that their dissatisfaction will be heightened. Of greater concern, though, is the reaction of parents who do not already harbor these feelings of dissatisfaction. What might their response to the suggestions of these titles be? Is it conceivable that without ever reading one word of the text, they might begin to question whether or not they have correctly been assessing their child's school? Might they, in fact, become less supportive and more suspicious, without any real basis for these attitudinal changes? Along the continuum of school supporters, with our most supportive parents on one end and our most difficult ones on the other, are there parents at any point who would have their opinions of our schools improved by glancing at these book titles? I think all of us agree that it's doubtful, at best.

Again, the content of some of these books may in fact lead to improved feelings of support from parents. If only the titles are read however, then such a result is highly unlikely. What we unfortunately wind up with instead is a growing segment of the population with distorted perceptions who claim that our schools are failing. We now face an increased struggle to correct these misperceptions. Remember, to many people, perception is reality. In our work as teachers, a major thrust of our efforts should be to positively alter people's perceptions of our classrooms and schools. It is very important to remember, though, that there are many people working against these efforts.

> *In our work as teachers, a major thrust of our efforts should be to positively alter people's perceptions of our classrooms and schools. It is very important to remember, though, that there are many people working against these efforts.*

Family Focus: Children or Adults?

In addition to examining the treatment schools receive from print and mass media in contemporary society, we should look again at the very structure and functionality of today's families. One way to assess these issues is to examine the subtle changes society has seen in parenting practices. According to some social psychologists, families can be classified as being either child centered or adult centered. In reality, most families certainly exhibit behavior from both classifications. Child-centered families, often represented by the middle class, are recognized as those families that focus their resources on the needs of their children. By contrast, adult-centered families, typically thought of as lower class or underclass families, tend to use available resources to satisfy the needs of adults, not children. It is important to note that economic classifications of families do not necessarily dictate whether they are child centered or adult centered. There are tendencies as we have mentioned, however.

Rather than judging all adult-centered behavior, we need to understand that in some cases, an adult-centered attitude grows out of a difficulty coping with the demands of daily life.

Rather than judging all adult-centered behavior, we need to understand that in some cases, an adult-centered attitude grows out of a difficulty coping with the demands of daily life. These adult-centered, or self-centered, parents spend much of their time worrying about basic needs, such as food and shelter. Consequently, children and the things they need are often pushed to the rear. This causes children to not have as much attention paid to their academic needs as they would have if they were in child-centered families. The result is less parent involvement at school, lower expectations, and poorer achievement. On the other hand, when families have the resources and/or the desires to be child centered, then the needs of the children become a focal point in family life.

In your own school experiences, you have probably seen these descriptions played out numerous times. Depending on the population served by your school, most readers have probably struggled with adult-centered families. As a result, many readers have probably complained from time to time that parents do not seem to care about their children. We need to understand that for some, but not all, of these families, there simply is no alternative.

Both of us authors can recall times when our hearts have been broken upon the realization that some of our students were not receiving adequate attention at home. Such thoughts as "If I could just take this child home with me . . ." or "Why don't these parents care?" crossed our minds, as they have crossed the minds of many of you. Difficult though it may be, we all need to realize that the apparent lack of care shown in adult-centered families is often masking a deeper problem. For many of these families, though clearly not all of them, there really is no choice.

It is also worth noting here that child-centered behavior can be taken to extremes that are equally as damaging as adult-centered behaviors are when they are taken to extremes. Recalling some of our own experiences, we can certainly remember parents who overindulged their children and became, in some cases, our most difficult parents to work with. The overindulgence experienced by their children created an unrealistic sense of self, which sometimes led to the child getting into serious trouble at school. The parents, expert at overindulging the child, always defended the child's actions, even when the child was clearly wrong. Have you ever had experiences like that? These, too, can be difficult to deal with.

Negative School Experiences

As teachers, we must be mindful of the fact that many of our parents did not have positive experiences when they were schoolchildren. In fact, attending school during an era that placed less emphasis on affective education than contemporary schools do, many of these parents do not view schools as places that concern themselves at all with the feelings and attitudes of the students. Also, in light of the many changes that have taken place in regard to the education of children with special needs, many parents still remember back to the days when schools were not quite so sensitive about different abilities. The only opinions that really mattered in determining a student's educational goals were those of school personnel. These parents, therefore, are not used to having their opinions count in educational settings. Despite the cries from our schools asking for parent involvement, many parents are skeptical about our sincerity. They suspect that their presence makes us uncomfortable, and that we would be just as happy if they stayed home and let us do our jobs. The cause of these negative school experiences is irrelevant. It makes little difference whether a parent views school negatively because of their own lack of effort to succeed or because of their perception that school failed them. The importance lies in the fact that the mere mention of the word "school" conjures up negative images for some of our parents.

> *Despite the cries from our schools asking for parent involvement, many parents are skeptical about our sincerity. They suspect that their presence makes us uncomfortable.*

*Many parents who do view
schools favorably and who
do believe our invitations
for involvement are sincere
become disenchanted by
the ritualized systems that
we have created for their
involvement.*

Many parents who do view schools favorably and who do believe our invitations for involvement are sincere become disenchanted by the ritualized systems that we have created for their involvement. Although many schools, as is outlined in later chapters, do provide new and different ways for parents to be involved, many are still mired in the traditional rituals we disguise as parent involvement opportunities. Consider, for example, the traditional open-house program in which parents are urged to come to school to listen to teachers explain rules and expectations for the school year. Usually, there is little opportunity for interaction between parent and teacher. This lack of interaction can cause an unintended gap to be created between teacher and parent, thereby reducing the chance that the parent will choose to be involved in future school activities. As Sara Lawrence Lightfoot (1978) acknowledged decades ago:

> Schools organize public, ritualistic occasions that do not allow for real contact, negotiation, or criticism between parents and teachers. Rather, they are institutionalized ways of establishing boundaries between insiders (teachers) and interlopers (parents) under the guise of polite conversation and mature cooperation. Parent-Teacher Association meetings and open house rituals at the beginning of the school year are contrived occasions that symbolically affirm the idealized parent-school relationship but rarely provide the chance for authentic interaction. (pp. 27–28)

Schools, therefore, need to examine the procedures that they have in place for encouraging parent involvement. School leaders and teachers need to structure activities that make it easier and more natural for positive interaction between parent and teacher to take place. Teachers need to be supportive of these efforts, ever mindful of the benefits students will experience as a result.

While there are plenty of difficult parents who appear not to care about their children's education, it is important to remember that many parents from all kinds of backgrounds do care about the education their children receive at school. Additionally, they do support the efforts of the school and recognize the significance of their role in the educational process. However, teachers are well served to realize that the diverse backgrounds of some of our parents creates a necessity for us to educate them about the importance of their involvement.

We speak openly in many of our schools about the need to be "diverse" or "multicultural." Yet, as we have observed, in many schools the dominant culture still rules supremely. Caring teachers must recognize that involvement and specific roles and responsibilities mean different things in different cultures. Consider the perception of many Asian immigrant parents. Due to cultural differences, many of these parents view communication with teachers as "checking up on them" and as an expression of disrespect (Yao, 1988). As a result, what appears to be apathy is more likely, in these cases, to be a sign of respect. Other cultures hold similar views. Unless they receive sincere, personal invitations to become involved, many parents will continue to stay away, not out of disdain, but out of respect. We all need to recognize this.

Angry Parents

As most veteran teachers can attest to, there are some parents who appear to be just plain angry. They may be angry for a variety of reasons, including some of those already mentioned in this book. As teachers, we are trained to search for answers to these and similar problems. We do this to a fault at times. Analyzing angry parents may be a perfect example. Rather than trying to understand precisely what it is that makes some parents angry with us, we need to look for ways to deal with their anger for the benefit of our students. If our goal in dealing with an angry parent is to understand why they are angry and then to convince them

Rather than trying to understand precisely what it is that makes some parents angry with us, we need to look for ways to deal with their anger for the benefit of our students.

not to be angry, we are often doomed to failure. Let's instead focus on better ways to deal with the anger itself. As Stephen Covey says in describing an important habit of interpersonal effectiveness, "Seek first to understand, then to be understood" (Covey, 1990, p. 255). In doing so, we will find ourselves defusing more situations and ensuring that our focus in all conversations with parents is what's best for their children.

In future chapters, we will discuss some specific techniques for dealing with angry parents. For now, consider this tale:

> On a path that went by a village in Bengal, there lived a cobra who used to bite people on their way to worship at the temple there. As the incidents increased, everyone became fearful, and many refused to go to the temple. The Swami who was the master at the temple was aware of the problem and took it upon himself to put an end to it. Taking himself to where the snake dwelt, he used a mantra to call the snake to him and bring it into submission. The Swami then said to the snake that it was wrong to bite the people who walked along the path to worship and made him promise sincerely that he would never do it again. Soon it happened that the snake was seen by a passerby upon the path, and it made no move to bite him. Then it became known that the snake had somehow been made passive and people grew unafraid. It was not long before the village boys were dragging the poor snake along behind them as they ran laughing here and there. When the temple Swami passed that way again, he called the snake to see if he had kept his promise. The snake humbly and miserably approached the Swami, who exclaimed, "You are bleeding. Tell me how this has come to be." The snake was near tears and blurted out that he had been abused ever since he was caused to make his promise to the Swami. "I told you not to bite," said the Swami, "but I did not tell you not to hiss."

In examining the many messages of this story, we can come to an understanding of anger and the responses it requires.

First of all, let's examine the emotional state of the cobra. In completely suppressing his anger, he wound up getting taken advantage of and walked all over. This is why many parents are unable and unwilling to completely suppress their own anger. It is also why we, as teachers, don't always completely suppress our own angry feelings. Human nature and what we have all learned about sound negotiation strategy has left us fearful of being taken advantage of. However, as your own experience has surely demonstrated, becoming angry with an angry parent rarely does any good.

Next, consider the Swami's final statement to the cobra. When he says, "I told you not to bite, but I did not tell you not to hiss," he is explaining that there are appropriate ways to show our emotions. Parents who lash out at us in verbal abuse are obviously "biting." This behavior is inappropriate and need not be tolerated. In fact, if a parent does engage in inappropriate, abusive behavior, then we have a responsibility to make it clear that such behavior is unacceptable. In upcoming chapters, we give specific advice on just how to do this. On the other hand, those who question us and show disapproval toward some of our decisions are merely "hissing." We need to know the difference. In knowing the difference, we must also take care to be less sensitive when we are being hissed at. We also have a responsibility to assist those who are biting to learn to hiss instead. Finally, we must take care to never bite back.

It is perfectly normal for us to wish that parents would not get angry with us or be so difficult. In fact, it's safe to assume that no teachers enjoy having people angry with them. It is also normal for us to yearn for the day, real or imagined, when parents did not ever show us angry feelings. In accepting reality, though, we understand that some parents are angry. This anger, whether we like it or not, will be expressed. We need to act as the Swami, insisting that parents hiss instead of bite, and acknowledging that anger does need to be expressed sometimes. The importance is in both the appropriateness of the expression and in our method for dealing with it. In Part II, we address important considerations for communicating effectively with parents. Parts III and IV provide a great deal of practical advice for dealing with angry or difficult parents.

Part II

Communicating with Parents

4

Building Credibility

Everyone Wants to Associate with a Winner

It is amazing what an incredible thing trust is. If we trust someone, they can tell us almost anything and we will believe them. By the same token, if we don't trust someone, they can tell us almost anything and there is not much chance we will believe them. The same thing is true regarding our relationship with the parents of the students in our classes. If we can establish trust with them, they will allow us great discretion in decisions that we make. However, if they do not trust us, then they inspect everything we do with a high-powered microscope. Knowing this, how can we develop that bond with parents so that at the very least we can get the benefit of the doubt? Is there a way to nurture that relationship to the degree that we can develop a culture and spirit of mutual regard, which will allow us a much wider swath of trust? It can happen in all schools with all educators, but it is definitely something that we have to work at.

If They Don't Hear Good News from You

One of the first challenges that teachers and schools face is developing a positive image. Unfortunately, oftentimes the newspapers, radio talk shows, and many political officials will take potshots at educators and the profession itself. Part of this is because they hear other people do it. Once, on a sports radio call-in show, a 9- or 10-year-old boy called in criticizing a former St. Louis Cardinal catcher named Ted Simmons. The boy lamented, "Simmons is lazy. He can't hit, he can't run, he can't throw, and he was a bad influence on the team! In addition, he is way overpaid and a bad role model in the clubhouse."

The wise talk-show host said, "It sounds like somebody has been listening around the supper table." Well, we think it sounds like a lot of people have been listening around the water cooler. We all see ourselves as educational experts simply because we all went to school. How does the old quote go? *If we took every critic of education and laid them end to end . . . they would be a lot more comfortable.*

We also know that people in general view their local schools in a much more favorable light than they do schools on a national basis. Additionally, parents view the schools their children attend more positively than do community members without children in school. With this in mind, what can we do to build credibility and trust with all of our constituents?

Everyone Wants to Associate with a Winner

Understand that everyone wants to associate with a winner. If you ever question it, just look at your local college basketball team. The team that struggles the most needs more fan support than ever, but seldom does this occur. Instead, the most successful teams tend to consistently pack the house. It is interesting, but there aren't nearly as many Miami Heat fans since LeBron James returned to Cleveland as there were when he was still playing for Miami and the Heat were winning!

With this in mind, how can you best spread the message that your school or your classroom is a winner? Let's start with the basic notion of open-house or back-to-school night. What do you and your school do to promote the event? Does your student council have an evening in which they attempt to call every single family and personally invite them to back-to-school night? Regardless of the size of the school, you could develop a short script for the students to read in which they encourage every family to attend back-to-school night. Set a goal so that every household receives one phone call inviting them to open-house night. If the students receive an answering machine when they call, then they leave a message. If no one answers, then they move to the next one on the list.

This could be done much more easily with an automated calling system, but does that accomplish the same concept as a personal invitation? Maybe an automated call is the approach needed on a school-wide basis, but on a classroom level, something more personal might be more appropriate.

Moving from a school-wide basis to an individual teacher basis, you could personally call the parents of every student you have and invite them to attend. If you are in a departmental setting with vast numbers of students, then perhaps you could get a few parent volunteers or students to assist. We realize this is a lot of work, but it is amazing how it will reap rewards.

In addition, individual classrooms could hold a contest to see which homerooms have the largest percentage of students represented. In other words, if a homeroom has 30 students and 18 of the students have at least one person attend back-to-school night, they would have a 60 percent representation. Regardless of whether students had one, two, or five people from their family attend, it would still count as one student being represented. Then, the principal, teachers, or parent volunteers could serve donuts to the winning homeroom the next day. If you could not get the school-wide organization going, then there could be a contest among a grade level, team, or department. Obviously, what we do when we get them there is the next step.

Understand that regardless of whether we have 20 or 1,000 people come to our open house, we need to make sure that the ones that do attend feel special. *Do not* focus on the people who are not there. Instead, make sure that the ones who did come have a very positive feeling about their attendance. Make sure that you warmly greet everyone that you see. If the parents can have an initial positive impression of you, that can help temper future issues that may arise. Even more important, if they develop a negative impression of us, that may be difficult, if not impossible, to overcome. Having open house as early as possible in the school year or even right before school starts may be the best timing. No one has "been in trouble yet," and we are

Making a positive impression before we would have to deliver bad news is essential in building trust. It is essential that we build a relationship before we need the relationship.

all still undefeated. Making a positive impression before we would have to deliver bad news is essential in building trust. It is essential that we build a relationship before we need the relationship.

Chapter 5 provides some specific ideas on ways to make those positive contacts. One thing to keep in mind is that if we suspect that at some point we might have to deliver bad news to a parent, we might want to make it a special point to deliver good news quickly so that the positive interaction can be our first contact and impression with them.

Here is another idea for open houses that we have found to be simple and yet very effective. When I was a principal, in front of the entire auditorium full of families, I would tell parents to call me anytime—at school or at home. I would then tell them my home phone number is in the book and if they want to write it down it is 555–8493. It was amazing the stunned looks that would appear on the parents' faces when we did this. If you were a parent in the auditorium, how would that make you feel?

The first time we did this at open house night, a faculty member asked how I could possibly encourage people to call me at home like that. I replied, "The few irrational parents we have can always find your home number, and they will call you at home regardless. However, this approach makes everyone in that auditorium feel that someone cares about them and their child." Years later, parents would tell me that they always remembered that. The other benefit, of course, was that numerous teachers in the school would see it and then follow this role-modeled behavior. Throughout the school, I would observe that teachers would write their home phone numbers on the board in their classrooms. Whether or not the school principal chooses to do this, each individual teacher can still use this approach with the parents of their students to help establish trust.

If you are the only teacher in a school who does this, it really establishes a positive differential between you and other staff members. It can go a long way to building the relationships that are essential during the school year.

I can imagine that you are thinking to yourself that you already receive too many phone calls at home. Relax, you will not receive more calls at night. As a matter of fact, I think I received fewer. I had numerous parents tell me, "I was going to call you at home. I know you said we could, but I figured you get so many calls that I decided that I did not want to ever bother you at night." They felt better about me, and I actually had more of a personal life. This exact approach is just as appropriate and effective in each individual classroom setting. Every teacher can build and grow a higher level of trust with the parents of their students by using this approach.

Let Me Introduce Myself

Another technique that we can use in our classrooms is to call every student's household before school starts and introduce ourselves to the student and/or the parents. You can say something as basic as, "Hi. I'm Caroline Jones and I will be DeJuan's fourth grade teacher this year. I am really looking forward to having him in class and I just wanted to call and introduce myself." You could also ask if they have any questions or you could tell a little bit about your personal background. If the open-house night is coming up, you could combine this call with an invitation to attend.

A similar activity would be to have a "Welcome back to school!" picnic for the students and parents. You could send postcards announcing the date, time, and place and even ask people to bring a dish to share. Starting with positive contact can help establish a very productive relationship with parents.

Touching Base

Not only is the idea of touching base a good idea at the start of the year, it is equally effective at any time during the year. Calling one or two families a week can allow us to spread out the work and still touch base. Just asking a

Just asking a parent in October how things are going so far can be of great benefit throughout the year and help solidify the trust that we have established.

parent in October how things are going so far can be of great benefit throughout the year and help solidify the trust that we have established.

Another effective technique is that if you have a parent who has expressed concern over a situation, touch base with that parent a week or two later to ask how things are going. It is especially fun to do this when you know things are going better. You might ask the student how everything is going in regard to the previously troubling situation. After he or she shared that things were going great, you could then call his or her parents and ask for their perspective. Though you might already know what the answer would be, the real benefit is to show care and concern toward their child. This can have a long-lasting and positive impact. And since things really were going well, it is a chance to have a positive contact with the parents. This would be doubly important if you felt this was going to be a challenging parent to work with or if they happened to be married to a school board member!

Reaching Out to the Community

Making a positive impression throughout the whole community is important too. Consistently contact local television and radio stations as well as print media outlets with every piece of good news that you can think of. And if they ignore you? Then just keep after them. Find out if you have any parents with media contacts or if your business partner may have access. This is something that can be done on an individual-teacher or whole-school basis.

Another way to reach out and potentially get positive recognition is by doing community service projects. Your class could adopt a local nursing home or do a service project by cleaning up a local park. An athletic team you coach could go to a retirement center and sing Christmas Carols to the group. I used to do this with my varsity boys basketball team, and it was amazing how beneficial this was for the team as well as for the community. When you do special projects like this, make sure that you inform the media and put it in your school classroom newsletter. Coupling the positive experiences with beneficial publicity is an important facet of building up credibility.

Obviously, we can circumvent or supplement traditional media outlets by using social media to promote all of the positive things that are occurring in our classroom and school. We will go into more detail later in the book, but this approach using a class/school Twitter, Facebook, Instagram, etc. account allows you to be in control of the messages being sent to parents and the community.

My News Is Good News

Many classrooms and schools have regular parent communications. In addition, many classroom teachers, middle school teams, or high school departments have monthly, weekly, or even daily newsletters that are routinely shared with parents and families. These tools are an important way to make sure that we represent ourselves and our roles in the most positive light possible.

One thing that is so critical in a newsletter, memo, or any other correspondence that goes out to the masses is to make sure that we constantly focus on the people who are doing things right, not those who are doing things wrong. Do not send correspondence to all parents when only two do not pick up their children promptly after basketball practice. Understand what happens with this approach. People are already aware that they should pick up their children promptly; it is just that some forgot or maybe even don't care. Realize that those parents either will not read the communication, cannot read it, or do not care even if they do read it. Instead, the 95-plus percent of parents who are responsible are left with a negative taste in their mouths because of the tone of the piece. Additionally, reminding people at the end of an event what they had *better* do the next time is fruitless at best.

Instead, work on preventative maintenance by issuing friendly reminders with parents prior to field trips and other events. We realize that will not always work, but at least we are not insulting all of the positive and responsible parents in our school.

5

Taking Your Classroom Social

A tremendous number of teachers use social media as a communication tool. Teachers post pictures on Instagram, connect with friends via Facebook, and tweet their thoughts on a regular basis. However, often they may do this more as private citizens and not in their capacity as teachers. In fact, some schools still even have very definite policies regarding whether or not teachers can use social media tools in their roles as school employees. However, if allowed, we urge you to use social media in your role as a teacher to communicate positively, widely, and effectively with parents. Used appropriately, social media is an incredible tool for communicating with lots of parents in a simple format. It needs to be done carefully, but many, many teachers are able to do so effectively, and they find that social media is a fantastic and useful communication method.

While once reserved for the cutting edge, high tech among us, it has become almost necessary for teachers to utilize social media as a communication tool with parents. Traditionally, all school communications, particularly those involving parents, have been all about managing the flow of information and then framing the discussion about that information. It has been done via school newsletters, emails, postcards, and the like. But in today's world, where we're enriched with so much media

41

and technology, things have changed. Popular social media tools like YouTube, Facebook, Twitter, Vine, blogs, and webinars enable schools to maintain interactive dialogue with parents, students, and community members. Today, the purpose of communicating with parents is not just about information sharing. Instead, it is all about building relationships. The interactive nature of these tools is actually all about this. Social media is the simplest, most practical way to build relationships with large groups of people.

Today, the purpose of communicating with parents is not just about information sharing. Instead, it is all about building relationships.

It can also be the simplest and best tool available for sharing good news with parents and the larger community. As Whitaker, Zoul, and Casas say in *What Connected Educators Do Differently* (2015), we need to take advantage of this tool so we can ensure the right information gets shared about our school. They explain:

> With the tools available to us now, it is easy to take the lead in ensuring that the story that gets told about our schools and our school districts is a story that is accurate and focused on the major, not the minor, happenings. How we share information can affect our school environments both positively and negatively. As the storytellers for our students and our schools, it is critical that we understand our role and intentionally plan how we communicate and share our story in a way that shows the pride we have in our school and our entire school community. (p. 40)

Is Everybody Doing It?

If you need to be convinced about the widespread use of social media in our society today, consider these points. More videos are uploaded to YouTube in 60 days than the combined number that NBC, ABC, and CBS have produced in 60 years. How many readers know that the U.S. Library of Congress has archived every tweet ever sent via Twitter? At press, that represents more than 200 billion messages. When this book went to press, the top five social media sites had more than 2 billion followers. Increasingly and rapidly, most people have ditched their simple cell phones and begun using smartphones. In 2014, more than two-thirds of Americans used smartphones. Smartphone users check Facebook, a tool that was once thought to be a passing fad, an average of 14 times a day. Within 10 minutes of waking up, 81 percent of smartphone users check social media (statistics from www.iacp-socialmedia.org/Resources/FunFacts.aspx). We admit that we are among those with this lifestyle habit. In short, social media is pervasive.

In the time it takes you to read this book, at least five more teachers will open or begin using Twitter accounts. Twitter, in short, is the fastest growing social media outlet for getting information out to large groups of followers. While it's easiest to measure the impact of Twitter by looking at the number of people using it, it's more significant and useful to examine how much more sophisticated its use has become. Just a short while ago, people logged on to Twitter so they could follow celebrities and read their humorous comments. Soon after, though, great teachers began using Twitter to grow their professional and personal networks and to put out information for others to view at their convenience. Twitter, in short, has become an incredible communication tool that costs nothing but impacts an endless number of people. Back when we were classroom teachers, there simply was nothing, real or even imagined, that could do this.

In addition to being such a useful tool, Twitter is one of the easiest social media tools to master. Essentially, these are only a few main things to consider:

1. Whatever you want to say needs to be said in 140 characters or less.

2. Pictures can easily be attached to tweets. Once attached, they all appear in the same format—pic. twitter.com

3. Hashtags (#) are used to provide links to other tweets containing the word or words listed immediately after the hashtag.

So, if you are not already using Twitter to communicate and broadcast messages to parents and/or other community stakeholders, you really should consider beginning.

A Twitter Classroom

No matter your grade level or discipline, just think of the valuable communication tool Twitter can be in your classroom. As you read this book, there are teachers across the country that are tweeting at the end of the school day short messages that parents can view pertaining to homework assignments, enriched learning opportunities, or important reminders. Taken further, there are teachers sending out tweets during their lunch hour that celebrate individual class accomplishments or that simply contain positive messages about school. Just imagine parents' reaction when they read tweets like those below:

♦ Today, my students really brought their A game.

♦ So proud of my students!

♦ Teaching is the greatest job in the world!

♦ We love learning about Columbus! pic.twitter.com/ ####

♦ Every student turned in their homework today!

Teachers also can appoint students to be the official class tweeter. Using the account set up for the teacher or for the class, the selected student could post the pictures or write the tweets. In this way, Twitter becomes a common tool shared by all members of class community. Don't forget that parents are even more likely to follow a teacher or a class on Twitter if they know that their child may be the one writing the tweets or taking the pictures to attach. The quickest way to grow your local teacher network in your community is to include students in your tweets.

Initial Considerations

As you think about the best ways to use social media tools with parents, make sure that you consider what the purpose is of these tools in the first place. Most times, social media works best when the teacher has actually thought about her purpose for using it. Here are some things you need to consider before jumping in:

♦ What is the current state of affairs in terms of your relationship with parents? What are parents and community members already saying about your school?

♦ What steps do you need to take to build trust and a sense of community? How can you leverage what people are already saying to help develop a sense of community?

♦ Once you've built trust and community, it's easy to ask parents to support fundraisers, volunteer for school activities, or become members of your school–parent group.

♦ With a few strong parent relationships, you can get commitments from your inner circle of parent leaders to comment and share school messages on Facebook and Twitter.

♦ Add Facebook and Twitter links to all emails and handouts from the school and parent group to facilitate wider participation.

♦ Create a *social media plan* for big events like the school carnival, fundraisers, academic fairs, family cleanup days, and membership drives. What messages do you want your parent community to share? What actions do you want them to take? Write suggested Facebook posts and Twitter messages and share them with your inner circle of parent social media leaders.

♦ Add a Facebook "like" box and a "follow us on Twitter" button to your school or classroom website.

The main reason for doing this in the first place is to help build a very broad community of parents, teachers, and volunteers who are engaged and willing to become involved and support your school. Once parents start joining your online community (on Facebook and Twitter, for example), listen and engage with them. Build rapport and trust so they stick around, invite their friends, and take positive actions for your school! Remember, if parents don't typically, or ever, use the social media tool that you use, they quickly will once they realize that the tweets may feature their own kids and their accomplishments. Nothing recruits people to Twitter, Facebook, or Instagram more quickly, for example, than the thought that they might be featured in some way!

> *Once parents start joining your online community (on Facebook and Twitter, for example), listen and engage with them. Build rapport and trust so they stick around, invite their friends, and take positive actions for your school!*

Remember to Use Good Judgment

There are cautionary tales about social media, but they typically involve teachers who failed to use good judgment. The cautionary tales involve teachers who have improperly used these social media outlets and/or violated school policies. In each case described below, the situation was entirely avoidable. While we don't want to dwell on the negative, consider these examples:

In 2015, a Florida parent discovered a Facebook discussion among teachers of her child's elementary school in which one teacher called a student the "evolutionary link between orangutans and humans." Another teacher responded that the comment made her "laugh out loud."

In 2014, a first grade teacher in New Jersey was suspended after writing on Facebook that she felt like a "warden," and referred to students as "future criminals."

Also in 2014, a Pennsylvania teacher was suspended for blogging about her students and referring to them as "disengaged, lazy whiners."

While we need to be aware of the consequences of negative usage, we needn't fear those consequences. Great teachers use great judgment all the time, every day. The examples on page 46 simply are not examples of good judgment at all.

The only other consideration to be mindful of is that privacy settings on social media tools are not entirely foolproof. People often fail to remember how easy it is for unintended people to read their social media posts. Some people become nervous by this fact, but again, we say that using good judgment about what to post negates this concern. Even though you intend your social media communication with parents to remain within your defined community group, it doesn't matter if other people see it, as long as you use good judgment. Those among you who use social media as a communication tool with parents already know that there is nothing to fear, but a great deal to gain. Those of you who don't should consider trying it. It takes little time and produces great rewards!

A Few Practical Examples

While there are many great uses of different social media tools for teachers to communicate with parents, we'll close this chapter with a few practical uses for Pinterest, Twitter, and Facebook, as these are the most widely used and easily accessible via smartphone:

Pinterest

As a visual social media tool, Pinterest is all about the pictures. Users "pin" pictures to their "boards," so that other users with similar interests can see them and learn from them. It essentially is a thought and idea gathering place.

Teachers can pin pictures of their students engaged in a classroom activity or a field trip. They can post pictures taken from their Smart Boards so that students and parents can review lessons at home. They can post pictures of informational notes that previously were only communicated through copy paper and ink. Basically, if you can see it, you can pin it!

Twitter

Since tweets are limited to 140 characters, Twitter is a great tool for posting short, specific comments or directions. Also, remember that it is possible to set up your Twitter account so that only approved followers can view your tweets. However, you still should write them in a manner that you wouldn't mind the whole world seeing. Twitter can very easily and effectively be used to:

1. Share educational news and events that happened during the day;
2. Post reminders about upcoming events or alterations in the school schedule;
3. Share information from field trips or school activities.

Teachers can use Twitter in a private manner by tweeting directly to a parent of a nervous child to let that parent know how the child is doing during the day. In the old days, this required time to make a telephone call and hope that the parent was available to answer. With children who are on a behavior plan, building Twitter into the plan can let the child know that the parent and teacher are on the same page and in regular communication.

Facebook

Since so many people are on Facebook, you can use it to post information for a wide group of parents to see instantly. Facebook allows you to post updates that parents can see immediately when they log onto their page. You can post information about homework, to clarify a new policy, or to explain how students are to complete an assignment. Parents can also send you a private message to ask questions about homework or to ask for a meeting. Parents who might be uncomfortable asking questions in person might feel far more at ease when using Facebook.

Not only does Facebook give you an easy way to share class news and information with parents, but it also has some privacy settings that are easy to use. For example, you can create a private parents' group for your class and share information only with the parents of your students. By using the privacy settings, outside users should not have access to this information. Since you always use sound judgment however, that's not really a concern. Whatever you post on your class Facebook page will only pertain to the people that you are "friends" with, but if others see it, you have no concerns.

Parents are busier than ever, and their lives are far more complex than they used to be. Traditional methods of communicating with them lose their effectiveness more and more each day. We still really value positive telephone calls, emails, or postcards. In fact, great teachers increase, not decrease, their use of these communication tools. The world of social media has opened up so many doors that are easy to navigate, though. As most readers already know because of their personal use of these tools, we all can communicate with, inform, and stay in touch with people in ways that were unimaginable just a short while ago. We urge you to bring these tools into your professional life as a teacher. Parents will appreciate it, and the perception of you, as a teacher who regularly and purposefully communicates, will grow by leaps and bounds.

> *Parents are busier than ever, and their lives are far more complex than they used to be. Traditional methods of communicating with them lose their effectiveness more and more each day.*

6

Positive Communication with Parents

An Ounce of Prevention

One challenge that all educators face is building credibility with parents. We often hear from teachers and administrators that parents do not respect educators anymore. Stories are shared that when "we" were growing up, if the school called regarding misbehavior, when you got home there were follow-up consequences. Sometimes teachers lament that their word used to be "bond" and now there is little or no support at all from the families. However, even if it is true that educators no longer automatically have respect from all the parents, there is a way to build and nurture credibility even with the most challenging of families.

Positive Phone Calls

When I first became an assistant principal in charge of discipline and supervision at a junior high school, I remember looking at my job description wondering what the good things about my job were. I looked at the first page of the description and then turned it over and read the second page. After reading the entire document, I sat back and still wondered what the good things about my job would be.

I realized if I just waited for things to happen, I was only going to deal with students when they were in trouble, with teachers when they had a problem, and especially with parents when they were upset. Well, I knew this was no way to function or enjoy my job. I quickly realized I could get into classrooms regularly and be visible throughout the school. This would allow me to have some positive interaction with students and teachers and would assist me in beginning to establish credibility with them during neutral or positive times.

However, this still did not allow me to have positive interaction with parents. I knew that to do so was essential, basically because I would have to have a great deal of less positive contact when I called them with punishments, detentions, suspensions, and the like, as assistant principal responsible for the discipline of 700-plus eighth graders. Also, I was well aware that if the students went home and said positive things about me, then that would also help the parents think of me in a more positive light.

When I was an assistant principal, I realized that it was up to me whether I was going to enjoy my job or not. If I just waited around for things to happen, they surely would. Unfortunately, most of the things that come the way of an assistant principal responsible for discipline tend to be negative. I then determined that it is *my* responsibility to meld my job so that it would be enjoyable to come to work each day. In order to try to maintain a little balance in my job, I started a *positive referral* program.

Most schools have discipline referrals, where teachers "write up" kids for misbehavior and then send them to the office with the referral form. Assistant principals often deal with the majority of these situations. However, I felt that it was at least as important to have a positive referral program. This was a form that was similar in format, only we put it on bright red paper. Teachers would "write up" students for doing positive things. It could be that Tim got a B+ on a math quiz, they enjoy seeing Megan's smiling face every day, or Juan helped a student who was on crutches move around the school for a week. As long as it was something authentic, it was appropriate to write up a positive referral and put it in my mailbox.

When I pulled the positive referral out of my mailbox, I would send for the student. Initially, students were nervous, frightened, or defensive when they were summoned to the office. Often students would walk in and immediately tell the secretary, "It wasn't me!" When I called the student into my office, I would first congratulate them and tell them how proud I was of their accomplishment. I would share with them which teacher referred them and why they did so. I would thank them for their contribution to making our school a better place.

This in and of itself may have been enough and it definitely helped establish credibility and positive relations with students. However, I took it one step further. I would pick up the phone and call the child's parent. And if they had two parents, I would call the one that worked. If both parents worked, I would call the one that worked in the busiest office or on the most crowded factory assembly line. Let's think for a moment what those phone calls were like. Here is an example of a call regarding a positive referral with Kenny Johnson's mother at work.

"Hi. Mrs. Johnson, this is Bill Smith, assistant principal at Meadow Grove Middle School."

As you can imagine, this conversation was usually interrupted at this point by the parent with a loud moan, "Oh no!"

I would then continue with the conversation. "Mrs. Johnson, I am sorry to bother you at work, but I just thought you might want to know that Kenny's teacher, Mrs. Smith, is running around up here at school, bragging on your son. She sent me a positive referral saying that Kenny did an excellent job working with his group leading a science experiment yesterday. I called Kenny down to the office to congratulate him and I wanted to call and share the good news with you."

The conversation then would typically continue in a very positive manner and I would let the parent know that the student was in the office with me and that he or she was welcome to talk with them.

A lot of schools have positive referrals and other such programs. This is wonderful. However, the added twist of calling the parents at work led to several significant and positive contributions for me. Interestingly, the most frequent comment

I received from parents was, "A school has never called with anything good before." This was consistently the theme when I called hundreds and hundreds of parents. It did not matter if I was contacting the parent of a student who was frequently in trouble or the future valedictorian. Parents had never had unsolicited, positive contact from anyone at school.

Though I thought this was very sad, it did help me realize a couple of things. First, I finally understood why people believe the criticism of schools and teachers they read in the newspapers. I now was also able to comprehend why people buy into the nonsense that they hear on radio call-in shows criticizing educators and schools in America. It is because if they do not hear good news from us, the public may never hear *good* news about schools and teachers. Thus, it is critically important that we consistently initiate positive contact with parents.

At this point, you may be asking yourself a couple of things. "Why did you call parents specifically at work?" and "This is all fine and dandy, but what does it have to do with building credibility with parents?" Well, let me take a stab at both of those questions.

I called the parents at work for a very selfish reason. It relates to the publicity issue. When I called Mrs. Johnson and her initial reaction was a loud "Oh no!" do you have any guess what was the first thing she did in that crowded office when she hung up the phone after receiving good news? She told everybody in the office! I do not know about you, but I do not mind people saying good things about me and my school in public. I also know there was an office full of other parents who were thinking to themselves that their child's school never has called with good news. Anything that builds the reputation of you and your school does nothing but help parents see you in a more positive light. And your relationship with the parents is also greatly enhanced.

Additionally, there were a couple of other selfish benefits involved in this whole process for me. If I had previously initiated positive contact with a parent, it is amazing how that impacted future calls, especially if I had to call the parent at some future point with less than good news. Let's pretend I had to call Mrs. Johnson several weeks later over a discipline matter.

"Hi. Mrs. Johnson, this is Bill Smith, assistant principal at Meadow Grove Middle School."

And Mrs. Johnson would reply, "Hi. How are you today?"

At first, I was so shocked by Mrs. Johnson's friendly response that I would assume she had not understood me! But, eventually I would continue:

"Mrs. Johnson, I am sorry to bother you at work, but today Kenny was involved in an incident where he . . . (was fighting, sent to the office, etc.) and as a result he will be receiving . . . (detention, suspension, etc.)."

Then, Mrs. Johnson would respond by using the "f" word on me. She would say, "That's okay. I know you're *fair*. You call me with good news and you call me with bad news. You can call me anytime you want."

What I quickly learned was that making positive referrals may have seemed like additional work, but it really made my job easier. I had built relationships with parents that had significant positive impacts down the line. My job just became more tolerable. However, the real benefit from making positive phone calls was even more selfish. They also made me feel better about my job and more confident in interacting with parents.

Interestingly, the reaction to this approach was so positive that the local newspaper and television stations gave the positive referral program wonderful publicity. This helped the community and parents regularly see my school and me in a very positive light.

After two years of doing this as assistant principal, I became principal, and the entire faculty decided to participate by making one positive phone call a week. When we first talked about this at a staff meeting, we realized that very few of us had ever made positive contact with parents. We then came to the conclusion that because of this omission, the only contact we ever had with parents was negative. We also decided that, for the most part, we were afraid of parents. Since such a large percentage of the time when parents contact us it is for something less than positive, we gradually became hesitant or even reluctant to interact with and especially initiate contact with students' parents and families.

We also realized that, believe it or not, we did not really know how to praise or what we should say when we do call parents with good news. Let's first take a look at the components of praise.

Five Things That Help Praise Work

One of the challenges that all educators face is learning how to praise. That may seem silly, but often educators have spent their whole careers looking for what is wrong, pointing out errors, and focusing on mistakes. This is a part of being a teacher. However, an outstanding educator looks for opportunities to find students doing things right. One of the difficulties for many educators is truly understanding praise and being able to apply it on a daily basis.

Ben Bissell (1992) has described five things that help praise work. He feels that these are important elements in order for praise attempts to have the most positive effect possible. The five things Dr. Bissell indicates as characteristics of effective praise are authentic, specific, immediate, clean, and private. Let us apply these general characteristics to the specifics of building credibility with parents.

Authentic means that we are praising people for something genuine, recognizing them for something that is true. This is an important facet because the recognition of something authentic can never grow weary. Sometimes people state that they do not praise more because they feel that it will lose its credibility or become less believable if it happens too much. The way to prevent this is to make sure that it is always authentic. No one ever feels that they are praised too much for something genuine. Authentic does not mean that it is earth shattering or a magnificent accomplishment. Instead, the only requirement is that it be true. As educators, we have many opportunities to catch students doing things right. Remembering them, writing them down, and

> *As educators, we have many opportunities to catch students doing things right. Remembering them, writing them down, and then making it a point to share them with the parents of your students is essential in developing positive relations.*

then making it a point to share them with the parents of your students is essential in developing positive relations.

The second characteristic of effective praise is *specific*. The behavior we acknowledge often becomes the behavior that will be continued. If we can recognize students' positive efforts with specific recognition, then we can help them see specific areas of value. For example, you might acknowledge that a student gave forth an excellent effort in class or assisted another student who was on crutches. Specific praise also allows you to reinforce someone in an authentic manner. If you use specific praise, you can recognize everyone in your classroom or even in your school. Even students that are struggling can still be praised. You do not have to be dishonest and say they are the smartest student in class, or that they got the highest grade on a test, if they did not. Instead, you can identify those areas that did have merit and acknowledge them through praise to their parents.

The third item is *immediate*. This means recognizing positive efforts and contributions in a timely manner. This is especially true when we think of our more challenging students. We realized that it was essential to have positive contact with parents *before* we might need to make a negative phone call. Thus, when we had potentially challenging students in our classrooms, we made positive phone calls to their parents as soon as there were any behaviors we could reinforce. It was amazing, but we realized that this approach saved us much consternation and grief in dealing with this parent at a later date under less positive circumstances.

Even a first phone call just to introduce yourself and say that you are looking forward to having Jimmy in class this year can lay some positive groundwork for the future. We talk about additional ways to do this later in this chapter.

The fourth guideline for praise is *clean*. This is often a very challenging requirement for praise. The expectation that praise be clean is especially challenging for educators. Clean means a couple of different things.

- First, praise is not clean if you are issuing it in order to get the student or parent to do something in the future. In other words, it is important to compliment students because their efforts are authentic, not just because you are hoping that they will do something different tomorrow. It is important to remind yourself of this quite regularly, because if you do not, you will be tempted to discontinue praising because you feel it "did not work." An example of this would be if you call a parent with praise for a less positive student for the effort he or she used on a science experiment in class that morning, and then later in the week, the student is less than polite to you. Do not feel that these two events are linked. Oftentimes we take the less than positive approach of students very personally. Although our goal is to get them to be more productive, we need to be aware that more often their mood has much more to do with them and the way they feel about themselves than it does with you and how they are regarding you.

♦ The second requirement for praise to be clean is a very challenging one for educators: It cannot include the word "but." If we are trying to compliment a student and say, "Billy did a good job on his math quiz yesterday, but . . . his science homework was done very poorly," the individual we hoped we were praising will very likely only remember the part after "but," which was a criticism. It is very unlikely that he or she will be able to recall the attempted compliment. If we really mean to praise someone, then it is important that we divide these two events. If we had stopped with, "Billy did a good job on his math quiz yesterday," then this could have been an authentic, specific, immediate, positive, and reinforcing event for this student (and help establish relations with the parent!). The other part of the comment, "his science homework was done very poorly" may have no need for immediacy. Tying these two together reduces or even eliminates the value of the praise.

The fifth descriptor of praise is *private*. If in doubt, you can always give praise in private. Calling the parent of a student not only helps cultivate positive relations with the parent, but it is a private and personal way to reinforce the student's behavior.

Calling the parent of a student not only helps cultivate positive relations with the parent, but it is a private and personal way to reinforce the student's behavior.

What Do I Say When I Make a Positive Phone Call?

Establishing a particular approach to doing something that you are unfamiliar with or even uncomfortable with can be very helpful in building up your confidence to do it. I guess I first learned this approach when I was going to call a girl up and ask her out for a date. I would write down what I wanted to say and even a couple of other topics to bring up in case the conversation fizzled. Once I knew how I wanted to start the phone call, it gave me more confidence in actually dialing the phone. This same thing can be true if we are not used to initiating positive contact with parents.

Positive or negative, we always want to start all of our parental phone calls in the same manner. Everyone can meld an approach that works best for them, but having a place to start can go a long way toward building their skills. One way to start every phone contact, positive or negative, could be with this language: "Hi, Mrs. Johnson, this is Tom Walker, Kevin's science teacher at Smith Middle School. I am sorry to bother you at work (or home), but. . . ."

We will discuss delivering bad news in Part IV of this book, but for now, let's continue examining a dialogue appropriate for making positive contact with parents.

As a principal, making a phone call for a positive referral could go like this, "Hi, Mrs. Johnson, this is Tom Walker, assistant principal at Smith Junior High. I am sorry to bother you at work, but I just wanted you to know that Mrs. Martin, Kenny's math teacher has been running around here at school bragging on your son. She said that he got a B+ on his math quiz yesterday and that she was very proud of the hard work he put into preparing for that quiz." You could then go on to say you had a chance to call Kenny into your office earlier and congratulate him and let him know how much you appreciate his hard work. You could close the conversation by sharing with the parent that you are sorry you interrupted his or her work, but you just wanted to let him or her know what Mrs. Martin had said about Kenny in her positive referral.

For teachers, we would recommend a similar approach. Again, start each phone call to parents with the same language. "Hi, Mrs. Johnson, this is Karen Martin, Kenny's homeroom teacher. I am sorry to bother you at work, but I just wanted to let you know that Kenny did an excellent job leading his group in the science experiment this morning. He was very organized, and I really appreciated his efforts. I wrote him a note on his grade sheet telling him how proud I was of his efforts and, again, I did not want to bother you, but I just wanted to let you know what an excellent job he did this morning in class. Have a good day."

It is important to be very consistent in the way we interact with parents. Having a specific approach in how we initiate contact allows for a more level and diplomatic conversation, regardless of what kind of news we shared.

Different people might have different approaches, but it is important to be very consistent in the way we interact with parents. Having a specific approach in how we initiate contact allows for a more level and diplomatic conversation, regardless of what kind of news we shared.

One of the most powerful aspects of initiating the positive contact could be what you receive from the students the next day. One of the comments they share most frequently is how excited their parents were and how much they appreciated it. Amazingly, the age of the students is irrelevant. They all appreciate the positive stroking.

Do not ever underestimate the value of positive contact with parents. If you call them in September and if the next time you interact with them is April, they will often still remember and acknowledge how much it meant to them, even if your April contact was to inform them of something less positive.

You Mean I Got Something in the Mail Besides a Bill?

In addition to making phone calls, a similar approach is to send positive emails, postcards, or letters home to parents about something good that their child accomplished. Many teachers and schools do this on a regular basis. You could have postcards made that have a printed border in your school colors with the words or phrases "Wonderful!" "Terrific!" "Great Job!" or "Way to Go!" On the address side, you could print your school name and motto. Then any staff member could write something positive on the postcard regarding the student. (Keep in mind the five things that help praise work.)

You could then address and mail them to the parents. This is another way to not only reinforce positive student behavior, but also to enhance positive relations with all parents in the school. This may be doubly appropriate with students whose parents do not have phones or email.

When we first started sending the postcards, I wondered if secondary students even cared about this type of thing. However, I'll never forget that years after some students went through our school, if I went into their homes, I would see every postcard they ever received from their teachers still posted prominently on the family refrigerator. And I do believe that having the parents think positive thoughts about you, your class, and your school every time they get out the milk is probably very beneficial in establishing the relationship that you would like.

As a teacher, if you are the only person in the school who is doing this, you may have to use a standard postcard or generate a special letterhead on your computer that only you would use. As a principal, you could have these postcards printed up by the hundreds and regularly give them to everyone in the school: cooks, custodians, bus drivers, teachers, and other staff. It would help promote this activity even more if you could have office personnel or parent volunteers address the postcards for the staff so that it would be as easy as possible for the faculty. They could just turn in the postcards to the office, and then someone else would address the mailings.

The value of initiating positive contact can never be underestimated. Although it may be something that we are not familiar with, or that we have moved away from, there is no more effective way to build credibility with parents. It is essential that we do this as often as possible with the students and parents that have the most potential for future negative interactions.

> *The value of initiating positive contact can never be underestimated. Although it may be something that we are not familiar with, or that we have moved away from, there is no more effective way to build credibility with parents.*

Making sure to make positive phone calls and/or mail/ email messages can be a challenge for everyone. We always find time for whatever is most important, so we just have to decide that this is that important. Writing it down in your lesson plan book or calendar is often a productive way to do this. You could write in your calendar to make two positive phone calls every Tuesday and send positive postcards every Friday. Of course, this not only helps nurture positive relations with students and parents, but it also makes you feel good!

You Never Get a Second Chance

It is impossible to overestimate the goodwill that is generated by taking the time to make a positive first impression. This time and effort will be returned in a multitude of ways that will make your job easier and much more enjoyable. Teachers have such an impact every day. Sometimes we lose sight of how important and rewarding our profession is.

7

Listen, Learn, and Cultivate

Whenever we are talking to a group of teachers, a recurring theme seems to be the power of positive communication. Great teachers communicate positively every single day. Even when they are delivering bad news or correcting student behavior, the great teachers can do it positively. It can be challenging at times, though. The biggest challenge to positive communication arises when the individual we are communicating with is difficult. We surely all agree it is far easier to communicate with a positive person than it is to communicate with somebody who is difficult.

However true this may be, great teachers have the ability to communicate effectively with even the most difficult people. This communication, when handled in a productive manner, often has the power to defuse even the most *difficult* situation by winning over perhaps the most *difficult* person. To do so, teachers need to understand that relationships don't just automatically become positive. Difficult people can't simply become our allies or supporters just because we want them to. Instead, positive relationships with parents must be cultivated. We are reminded again of Stephen Covey's urgency that we "seek first to understand, then to be understood." (Covey, 1990, p. 255) We can do this with parents when we listen to their concerns, learn as much as we can about their perspective, and then begin to cultivate a positive relationship.

This idea of listening, learning, and cultivating relationships really boils down to having effective communication skills. Too many teachers think of communication with parents as being something they do primarily when there is a problem. This is partly due to the fact that, as teachers, we are all very busy people. It seems difficult to imagine having the time to communicate with parents when everything is going well. But as the best among us know, this is precisely the time when we ought to be communicating, particularly if our goal is to cultivate positive relationships with parents.

Communicating in Good Times

The best, most effective teachers are the ones who communicate with parents and all other stakeholders on a regular and consistent basis. Not only do they regularly communicate, but also they do it in a proactive manner. These teachers understand that communication will be ineffective if they always deliver it as a reaction or a response to a problem. This communication takes place when things are going well in addition to when things are not going so well. The least effective teachers, on the other hand, spend all of their communication time dealing with situations in which somebody did something wrong. These people seem to disappear during good times, only to reappear when somebody has done something wrong again. The effect this has on an already difficult parent or in an already difficult situation can be very damaging. Yet again, it's worth noting that teachers' busy professional lives can cause them to be reactive in their communication with others. But being proactive is required if we are to communicate with parents and other school stakeholders on a regular and consistent basis. The time to proactively communicate in a positive manner is right now!

Teachers' busy professional lives can cause them to be reactive in their communication with others. But being proactive is required if we are to communicate with parents and other school stakeholders on a regular and consistent basis.

If teachers only send home notes when students are failing or misbehaving, for example, then parents will quickly begin to dread hearing from teachers. We know that the thought of a parent dreading to see an email arrive from our email address or shuddering when they hear that we are on the other end of the phone depresses us incredibly. All of us entered the field of education to make a positive difference in the lives of children. Shouldn't we want people to be excited when they hear from us? Specific ways to make this excitement possible were discussed in previous chapters. Utilizing those techniques is essential if we want to cultivate positive relationships.

The most respected, effective teachers use varied forms of communication to regularly provide feedback to all stakeholders, especially parents. They contact parents with good news as often as they contact them with bad news. They use more formal means like regular newsletters or class web pages, as well as more casual ones like spontaneous telephone calls or conversations in the hallways. Though these educators do not hesitate to illustrate when something bad has happened or when something has been done incorrectly, they balance this with a healthy dose of positive communication. The result, more often than not, is a healthy relationship with parents.

Developing and maintaining healthy relationships with parents is vitally important to the success of any school. These healthy relationships come about through involvement and engagement of all parents. They do not come about in schools that alienate parents or communicate with them only in times of trouble. Here are three simple reasons why these healthy relationships are so important in the creation of positive school-home relationships:

♦ Schools that actively involve parents and the community tend to establish better reputations in the community.

♦ Consistent parent involvement leads to improved communication and relations between parents, teachers, and administrators.

♦ Students are more successful in school when their parents and school personnel work closely and cooperatively (Olsen, G. & Fuller M. L., 2010).

Education can be a difficult enough business. It is so much more difficult when we attempt to perform our duties without collaborative, supportive relationships.

Note the consistent theme in all three reasons: collaboration. Education can be a difficult enough business. It is so much more difficult when we attempt to perform our duties without collaborative, supportive relationships. Therefore, it makes no sense at all to fail to do all we can to collaborate with parents. As this section of the book has shown, communication is the key to building collaborative relationships.

We're Glad You're Here

It is essential that we do everything within our power to make parents feel welcome in our schools. It is amazing to note however, that many schools across the country blow the opportunity to do so immediately inside the front door of the school building. As an example, examine the policy that most schools must have nowadays that restricts visitor access by locking doors and forcing visitors to sign in at the main office before proceeding to another part of the school building. Though these measures may certainly be deemed necessary in the current environment, they still set a tone that we must work to overcome. We believe that the intended objective of these policies can be accomplished in a much friendlier and more welcoming manner than is currently done in many schools.

While these policies have become commonplace in our schools, the means by which they are announced and enforced differ from one another dramatically. In some schools, there are signs on the doors using language similar to the following: "Stop! All visitors must sign in at the office before proceeding farther." Many of these announcements are on posters shaped and colored to resemble stop signs. Is that more effective than the following example? "Welcome to our school! We are so glad that you are here! We do ask that all visitors please sign in at the office upon entering." Which message has a friendlier tone? Which message is more likely to make you really feel welcome?

Now, some may argue that the forceful language in the first example is necessary. Without such forcefulness, people would not listen. We, however, maintain that individuals who would ignore a message that says, "Welcome to our school! We are so glad that you are here. We do ask that all visitors please sign in at the office upon entering," are also more likely to ignore a more forceful message. In the meantime, by using a forceful message, we have unintentionally made some of our more positive parents feel unwelcome in our school because of the rather unfriendly edict that greeted them. The odds are that the same people will report to the office no matter how the message is delivered. Furthermore, from a safety standpoint, our hope is that if somebody has entered the school building with the intent to harm someone, they will do more than just visit the office. Our hope is that they will confess to the harm they are intending to cause. In this regard, visiting the office does not by itself make the school safer. It does create a feeling of safety, which helps alleviate the stress of some of our parents.

Another point to consider is the impact a negative greeting can have on a parent who rarely comes to your school. Because we are in our school buildings every day and we understand and regularly witness all of the positive things that go on in the school, an unfriendly greeting posted on the door doesn't seem like such a big deal to us. In fact, many teachers probably don't even notice these greetings on a regular basis. The parent who only ventures into your school once or twice a year is much more affected by these messages, though. This can't be forgotten.

The kind of welcoming greeting we are speaking of here goes beyond the sign that welcomes visitors upon entering the school. The entire atmosphere of the school's entryway must be considered here. A sign with a cheerful greeting placed in a dark and dingy entryway will do less to make a parent feel welcome than would the same sign placed in a bright and cheery entryway. Though we believe that the whole school should be attractively decorated, it is extremely important that efforts be made to make at least the entryway attractive. A very good technique for accomplishing this task is to involve or empower your parent organization. In this way, not only will the entryway be kept neat, clean, and welcoming, but also the very population you seek to welcome will feel ownership for the project's success.

Again, school safety is a real concern that we all share. It is prudent that we implement policies that will make our schools safer for all children. In doing so, we must maintain common sense, though. Schools can be safe and friendly at the same time. The welcoming greeting can be written so as to proclaim the importance of safety, but it can also contain helpful directions to the office and a sense that we really are welcoming our visitors.

Celebrating cultural heritages, diverse careers, and hidden hobbies and talents is one more way to say to parents, "We're glad you're here." Regardless of your school's grade levels, there are tremendous opportunities to welcome parents in to share some of their abilities and insights relative to their jobs or the ways in which their families celebrate holidays. Not only do these situations provide rich learning opportunities for your students, but they assist you in cultivating positive relationships with parents as you show them how much you want to learn from them.

There Is a Time and a Place for all Conversations

We all have our comfort zones. These comfort zones may be a simple location in the school building, or a favorite chair. Regardless, every one of us has a place where we like to have conversations with parents. We have places where we feel more in control and where we feel we are on our "home turf." We also all have mannerisms that we use to make us feel a higher degree of comfort in these conversations. What we sometimes fail to realize is that our comfort zone is often very different from the comfort zone of the parents we may be meeting with. By setting up the room before a parent conference in a way that makes us feel comfortable and in control, we often make the parent feel very uncomfortable. Without a doubt, this will lead a difficult person to become defensive and perhaps even more difficult.

There really is a time and a place for all conversations. Consider parent-teacher conferences. Although some teachers and some schools design these situations to meet everybody's comfort and communication needs, in many cases, all parent-teacher conferences look and feel the same. They feel as though the teacher is in control, and the parent is a visitor. This feeling is created in many instances by the way the room is laid out.

When teachers invite parents in for conferences, it makes no sense for the teachers to sit in their desk chairs while the parent is squeezed into a student's chair. This is particularly so for teachers in the primary grades. Mrs. Rodriquez is far less comfortable sitting in her 6-year-old's chair, for example, than she would be if she sat facing you in the same adult-sized chair that you were sitting in. With the negative feelings that some parents harbor before they even enter our schools, why would we intentionally exacerbate these feelings with the way in which we furnish and arrange the room?

There are other ways to make parent-teacher conferences more inviting and comfortable, and lots of great teachers regularly do them. They range from comfortable seating arrangements to refreshments being served, but the important thing to remember is to simply focus on how we make visitors feel. We find that by simply acting as you would if a guest came to your home, you can make the parent-teacher conference more inviting. You would never invite a guest into your home and then make them less comfortable than you are. In a professional environment like a parent-teacher conference, it simply seems like the environment some teachers create places them at a real disadvantage. Be mindful of that.

Similarly, we need to be mindful of the environment that is created during impromptu meetings with parents. Sometimes, we meet parents in public places, and they begin to ask us school-related questions or individual questions about their child. These situations, particularly when they take teachers by surprise, can be unnerving. But they don't have to be. Just as teachers never should intimidate parents by communicating in their classrooms from a position of power behind their desk while the parent squeezes into a student desk, parents shouldn't make teachers feel intimidated when they surprise them with questions in public. In these situations, it is wise to listen, be polite, and ask the parent to schedule a meeting with you. You can, and should, very kindly tell the parent that you are so excited to talk with them about their child's progress. Continue by pointing out that you'd hate to be overheard in public, and that you could be so much more specific if you had grades and materials in front of you.

There is a time and a place for all conversations. As teachers, we should always feel confident to create welcoming and equal environments that are most conducive to good, honest, and comfortable conversations.

The Wise Old Owl

When I was growing up, there was a framed saying that my parents had hung in our house. Its message has made an indelible mark on me. It said:

"A wise old owl lived in an oak. The more he saw, the less he spoke. The less he spoke, the more he heard. Why can't we be like that old bird?"

Heeding this message can help us a great deal, particularly when we deal with parents in difficult situations. Too often, we teachers make the mistake of thinking that our main purpose is to solve problems. We think that any angry or concerned parent that comes to us needs us to solve their problems. Sometimes, all we really need to do is listen. Sometimes, an upset person needs nothing more than to be listened to. We can't let our problem-solving disposition cause us to try to offer solutions in these cases. We have got to be judicious, and we all would benefit from remembering what the wise old owl did.

When we take the time to really listen, we can learn so much. When we learn, we are in a position to cultivate positive relationships. These positive relationships with parents will help us to achieve our mission so much more than negative relationships will. We simply need to listen, learn, and cultivate. This will form the necessary foundation for dealing with difficult parents.

Part III

Soothing the Savage Beast

8

Initiating Contact with Parents

One challenge we face is when we have to pick up the phone and start a conversation with a parent. This is especially true if it may not be received well or if it is a parent who may not be very receptive. Now you might be thinking, "Pick up the phone? It is much easier to email."

You are correct; it is easier. But it may not be better. When you email you now have shifted the dynamic so the other person is able to respond when they want to. And particularly if it is a worrisome situation or parent, it puts you in a position to fret.

Email or Call?

It may be tempting to initiate contact over email. If you have an established relationship with someone, this is probably fine. If you are sending neutral or positive information to a noncontroversial person, this may be totally acceptable. However, if you do not have an established relationship with someone or he or she is a more difficult person, it is important to heavily consider whether or not emailing is the way to go. This chapter goes into more detail on this, but a couple of things can happen if you email under these circumstances that may not have the best results.

The first is that you then may be worried until and about their response. This fretting stays with you because you are now dependent on how they will answer (if at all) and what they will say when they do. A second negative is they may wait to respond when they are most wound up. They have a chance to ask others what they should say, how they should say it, when they should say it, etc. Once again, it puts them in control. Now if they are a positive and supportive parent, no problem. But remember that if they are not, it may put us in a defensive posture. A third reason is now they have a "permanent" written record that they can cut and paste, share as they desire, post in social media, scour for typos or misspellings, and so on. The average, positive, and caring parent wouldn't use it for these purposes, but that is not who we are most worried about. If in doubt, pick up a phone and call. You have more opportunity to call when you are prepared, there is not a permanent record, and they have less time to plan than you do. Also, and maybe the best part, is that you can get it over with!

The Email Bomber

A follow up is how to respond to a parent who continually barrages you with email demands, complaints, or questions. This especially applies if it almost feels harassing or overwhelming. Remember that when anonymous people use social media, they feel greatly empowered to say horribly critical things that they would never say in person. Keep this in mind and take away the cloak of invisibility a person may feel typing into the keys of their computer or cell phone. If they communicate negatively in email, wait until you are ready and then call them. This more personal interaction on your part will likely make them feel less empowered. They wanted a feeling of "anonymity" by emailing, so make sure you do not continue to feed this by replying in the way they have chosen to communicate.

Less Talk, More Action

Don't threaten students that you'll call their parents. Just call the parents. Anytime we threaten to call parents, the students now have an opportunity to go home and prep their parents against you. If you tell students you are going to call their parents, the most challenging students will go home and tell their parents, "That teacher, who is always picking on me, may call you. I don't know why, but she said she was going to call everyone's parents. No one likes her anyhow!" Potentially you now have a situation where the parent may be accusatory or at the least have a slightly jaded view of what you tell them.

Now you may think that, of course, parents can see through this. And that may be true; however, you allowed a seed of doubt to possibly enter their mind by letting the student get in the first volley. Instead, if you just call the parents and the students have not prepped them in advance, you are much more likely to have the upper hand. It takes eight times longer to unlearn something than it does to learn something. If the student gets home first, the parent may never completely believe you. They should but they probably will not.

This same thing applies if you have the student call the parent during school, even if you are standing there listening. If the student tells the complete truth, this is a fine approach. However, what if the student says, "Mom, I am in trouble for talking too much in class. A whole bunch of other kids were doing it too, but I am the one that got in trouble. Here is the teacher if you want to talk to her."

If the student hands you the phone, you will potentially have to do damage control. Instead, call the parent while the student is there and share what actually happened, and then say, "Mrs. Smith, Kevin is right here if you would like to talk to him." The parents now know that they and their child heard the exact same story from you and it is much more difficult for either of them to be in denial.

If at all possible, make the first contact. That phone is our best friend, unless it is ringing.

> *If at all possible, make the first contact. That phone is our best friend, unless it is ringing.*

Who Do We Call First?

There are times when we may feel like one of our classes is out of control. It may be a particular group of students, a tiring/stressful time of year, or more likely some combination of these things. Pretend you have 25 students in class and the entire class seems like they are misbehaving and out of control. Many of us have felt this way at times.

Now, try to step back objectively and look at your roster of students in that class. Choose the nicest student in that class and ask yourself if he or she is out of control. The answer is most likely no. Then choose the second nicest student. Is he or she out of control? Keep going through your class seating chart. Let's pretend that it turns out that five of your students are out of control. Well, clearly that is a problem as we only have four corners in our room! Well let's imagine that we have tried everything and finally we decide to call parents. How many parents should we call?

You might think five, because there are five challenging students. You might think 25 because you want to call them all. You might think 10 because you want to call the five challenging students' parents and have five positive phone calls. There is no right or wrong answer for all settings. However, we would like you to consider this.

If you have five challenging students and one of them is absent, what is class like that day? It may feel like a holiday miracle. Even if it is one of the five students who is more of a follower than a leader, the dynamic may be dramatically altered and improved. With this in mind you might consider this.

If we have five challenging students, our goal is to go from five to four; then to go from four to three; then three to two, etc. There is very little chance of going from five to zero in one fell swoop. Always remember what your class is like when one of the five is not in attendance that day.

If we contact all five students' parents and it does not have the desired effect of changing the students' behaviors, potentially we have bonded the five students against us, and we do not want that to happen. Now, if it does have the hoped for impact then that is great. However, carefully think through your students. Is there a chance these five could be bonded against you? If so, proceed with great caution.

One suggestion might be to just call one parent. Though we might be tempted to call the parent of the leader, it may be better to call the parent who can most influence his or her child. Keep in mind our goal is to go from five to four. When that student becomes aware you contacted his or her parent, that student will immediately touch base with some jack-around buddies and find out you didn't contact the other parents. Then he or she will feel very alone and be much more likely to improve in behavior. Interestingly, the next members of the group who are likely to be influenced by their parents may also alter their behavior because they do not want to be next. Making sure you always have a strategy is essential if you want to improve student behavior by utilizing parental contact.

The Peak of Ready

We may be tempted to wait and build up our courage to call or contact a parent. We can hope it goes away on its own. However, many times when we do this, we worry and fret. Then sometimes we wait long enough and the student has arrived at home or called or texted a parent and then the angry parent contacts us. Now, what do we do?!

What has happened is by stalling, we let the parent contact us at their highest point of anger. They are the most prepared to be upset and let off steam. They are at what we like to call, "The Peak of Ready." They are at the point of being most upset and confident when they contact you. Even if earlier in the day, you were not positive what you were going to say to them and you may not have been your best, neither were they. If you think about how you feel when you get caught off guard and how inadequate to deal with this situation you are, this same advantage can be yours when you initiate the contact before the parent is dug in and fired up. Though by initiating contact, you will not be at 100 percent of your "Peak of Ready," you can pretty much guarantee that they will not be either. And by calling them at work or some other location when they may not feel as comfortable being verbose or disrespectful on the phone, you may add another layer enabling you to have a healthier and more productive conversation with a potentially volatile or challenging parent.

By being the initiator, you can make contact when you are ready, not when they are ready. Again, if you email bad news, the parent now is able to fire back a response when they are at their prime "Peak of Ready" moment!

Crying as a Weapon

We weren't sure exactly where to put this section but thought we might as well get it in now. Nobody repeats a behavior without a reward. In a later chapter, we discuss what if a parent says, "My child never lies to me." Along that line, we wanted to describe behaviors to be aware of when we initiate contact or even if we are not the initiator. As a teacher, at times you will have a parent who starts crying when you share bad news. Understand that some adults—just like children—will use crying as a weapon.

The first time this happens, you may be caught off guard and your natural caring and protective instincts will kick in. You may help them blow their nose, wipe their eyes and even help them reapply their runny mascara. This is completely fine. However, you need to remember the next time you are with them that they are criers. Nothing wrong with that—caring and sensitive people are wonderful individuals. Yet at times, some parents will do this so that you don't share bad news with them. You feel guilty, thus you soft step around giving them bad news about their child. This cannot happen. So, what do you do?

Like we mentioned, the first time you cannot be overly supportive. Reassuring them, giving them Kleenex, etc. are wonderful things to do. However, to make sure they are not using it is a weapon, gradually wean away your reaction. The second time you are with them have a box of Kleenex out but do not react to them crying. Continue the same caring and professional tone you would use if they were not crying, but don't respond to their tears.

If you meet with them again, have Kleenex a little farther away that they can help themselves to but they have to get up to retrieve them. If you meet with them regularly, eventually you might even get to the point where they have to wipe their nose on their own sleeve. We are almost kidding about this, but keep in mind that sometimes people revert to childhood behaviors

Keep in mind that sometimes people revert to childhood behaviors when reacting to a situation, and you should not let that prevent you from communicating professionally and appropriately.

when reacting to a situation, and you should not let that prevent you from communicating professionally and appropriately, even if you are communicating news they may not want to hear.

No One Wants to Initiate Contact with Challenging People

Initiating contact with potentially negative or volatile individuals is one of the least enjoyable parts of an educator's job. Even delivering bad news to nice people is no fun. Do not feel inadequate because you do not have a desire to do this. No one does. Keep in mind that there is not one educator in your school who wants to contact a negative parent. Just remember that the good people do it anyway. There is no difference in desire; there is a difference in action. Good luck!

9

Never Let 'Em See You Sweat

There is an old deodorant commercial that used the slogan, "Never let 'em see you sweat." The premise behind the advertising campaign was that in the rough-and-tumble business world, sweating was a sure sign of defeat. If you were involved in heavy business negotiations, and the opposition saw that you were perspiring, they would somehow realize that they had gotten to you. Now, they could move in for the kill. This premise went beyond television commercials and has been consistently repeated in movies as well. The confident "good guy" never sweats. In fact, those who sweat have traditionally been depicted as weak, frightened, lying, and on the verge of collapse. Yet, we both vividly remember times where the pressure of dealing with a difficult parent made us sweat and was really difficult to handle.

Despite the fact that difficult parents sometimes make us feel nervous or anxious inside, it is important that when dealing with a difficult parent, you never let 'em see you sweat. This is to say that as long as you appear confident and self-assured, even the most difficult parent's anger will be somewhat defused. As soon as your body language indicates that you are

> *As long as you appear confident and self-assured, even the most difficult parent's anger will be somewhat defused.*

unnerved however, then the offensive onslaught of a difficult parent may become pronounced. This will obviously put you at a distinct disadvantage.

What happens when you are a bit unnerved, though? How do you prevent yourself from sweating—either literally or figuratively? What if the difficult parent's anger really has taken you by surprise and made you nervous? By understanding a few simple techniques, you can appear confident. The appearance of being self-assured will pay huge dividends in the long run. We think that you will find that employing these techniques, when you're feeling really nervous or anxious inside, will really help you mask those feelings and appear confident and in control.

Lower Your Voice

If you think back to times when you were nervous, one of the places that this nervousness may have revealed itself is in the tone of your voice. When we are very nervous, there often is a shaky sound to our voice. We swallow a lot and our voice trembles as if puberty magically has descended upon us once again. These vocal intonations are obviously more pronounced when our voice is loudest. Therefore, to compensate for the shakiness, we simply lower the volume of our voice. Subtleties, such as a shaky quality, become much more difficult to realize at this point.

The lower vocal volume gives us another benefit, as well. Consider this illustration that we use when speaking to groups of teachers about classroom management. We usually ask the group to tell us some of the techniques they use for quieting an unruly group of students. Invariably, through the wide range of responses we receive from teachers in all corners of the world, somebody in the audience says, "I lower my voice until the only way that the students can hear me is to quiet down themselves." Usually, this leads others to recount tales of when they employed the same technique and received similar results. In fact, before long, many in the group begin realizing that this is among the best techniques for getting a roomful of noisy children to be quiet again. The fact is that many times people who are speaking loudly or boisterously only realize how ridiculous they sound when they have an opportunity to compare themselves with somebody else's quiet voice. At this point, their loudness becomes much more apparent and they begin to feel a bit self-conscious.

So if a very angry parent arrived at our classroom door unexpectedly and began yelling, or at least speaking with an exceptionally loud voice, we would greet and welcome that parent with the quietest voice we could muster. Of course, due to the fact that we were not expecting the parent, we might have felt a bit unnerved deep down. The quiet tone we used to communicate served two very important purposes for us, though:

1. It hid the nervous, shaky sound in our voice that might have put the angry parent at an advantage.

2. It served to quiet the angry parent's voice, as it showed the parent just how loud and boisterous he or she was being.

Increase Your Movement

Another trademark of a highly nervous, unsure person involves uncontrolled body movements like wobbling knees and shaking hands. While it was very rare for a difficult parent to make us feel this degree of nervousness, there were times when it did occur. Depending on the challenging parents that you work with and your own tolerance for confrontation, this may have happened to you as well.

When finding yourself visibly shaking, telling yourself not to be nervous and to stop shaking only seems to make the problem worse. Therefore, it can be very effective to actually *increase* many of your other body movements to make these uncontrollable ones less obvious. This increase in motion makes it appear as though you are trying to multitask while you are talking because of the many tasks that you need to complete. While listening to the parent, you can put things away that are lying on your desk, or you could pace behind the desk clasping your hands as if you are working through an important idea in your head. If these motions seem highly inappropriate for the moment, you might jot down a note or just tap your pencil a little bit. While these movements may appear rude, distracting, and uncaring if taken to an extreme, it really is better than the alternative of appearing to be a nervous person with wobbling knees or shaking hands. Remember, the goal here is to never let 'em see you sweat.

Just like when lowering your voice, there is an added, unplanned benefit to all of this movement. Oftentimes, the subtle movement can cause the difficult parent to become distracted, nervous, or uneasy. Though unintentional, you can subtly turn the tables on the difficult parent and start them on a path of nervous behavior. Also, as the parent follows your actions while you move around the room, you may gain back some degree of self-confidence. This, in turn, allows you to gradually stop moving, assume your position in your big chair behind your desk, and regain control of a conversation that clearly began with you being on the defensive.

Close the Gap

Think for a moment of a loud, boisterous playground bully you have dealt with before. This may be a student who is currently in your school, or it may be a bully that you had the displeasure of dealing with when you were a child. Regardless, think of the loudest, most threatening bully you can imagine. What happened whenever this bully started bellowing in a threatening manner? Our guess is that everybody backed away a few steps. This is a natural reaction and one that the loud, boisterous person often wants you to exhibit. When you don't exhibit this behavior, the bully gets confused. Therefore, another technique to consider when dealing with an angry parent who is acting like a bully is to close the gap and move a bit closer in proximity to the angry person.

This change in proximity must be done very calmly, while you are exhibiting open body language. It should be subtle but focused on the goal of moving you even closer to the other person, as unnatural as that may feel. Obviously, we would never suggest that you actually close the gap so far that you are "getting in someone's face." That type of behavior is way too confrontational and unnatural. Instead, the gap closing that we are referring to should be done ever so slightly and slowly. It is easiest to accomplish while you are talking, and it works best if you maintain eye contact. Simply making sure that you do not back away even slightly will help reduce the anger and confidence of the difficult parent. That, by itself can provide you some relief.

The Eyes Have It

A fourth technique in preventing difficult parents from seeing you sweat involves forcing yourself to look the difficult parent straight in the eye. Though difficult at first, particularly if you have been taken by surprise, looking a person directly in the eye gives you an air of self-confidence and self-assurance. More often than not, this technique has quickly turned things in our favor and put us in control of conversations throughout our educational careers. As stated earlier, we need to remember that many of our most difficult parents had many of their own negative experiences when they were students. As a result, many of them are much more intimidated by being in a school facility than they would initially like us to believe. Though this is certainly no cause for celebration and is actually a truth that we should hope to change over time, we need to understand the role it plays in the attitude parents often bring with them to school. Their anger, or the inherent need to protect their child from perceived harm, may lead them to your school with an air of confidence, but this confidence can quickly give way to a feeling of nervousness or apprehension if you employ the right techniques. Looking the parent squarely in the eye is one such technique. By looking an angry parent in the eye, we can convey a certain degree of understanding. More often than not, this will reduce the level of their anger. We can also show the parents that we are surprised by what they are telling us. Doing this with our eyes can help the parent to see

> *By looking an angry parent in the eye, we can convey a certain degree of understanding. More often than not, this will reduce the level of their anger.*

that comments such as theirs are unusual or unexpected. This may even cause the angry parent to calm down somewhat. If nothing else, looking a parent squarely in the eye shows the parent that you are listening. As we are well aware, this is often the only thing the difficult parent wants from us.

In some ways, the four techniques explained in previous sections may appear to be merely mind games that we play in difficult situations. Upon closer examination, they are really much more. They are proven strategies that will often prevent you from appearing to be nervous or weak. Remember, the purpose of all of this is to improve relationships with parents for the benefit of our students. A parent who comes into the school building with a problem and encounters a teacher who appears nervous at worst and uneasy at best is probably not a parent who is going to feel confident that their child's school is guided by strong, confident teachers. If we, as educators but not trained mediators, need to employ some calculated strategies to appear more confident, then are we really doing something bad?

Another point to consider is that the whole reason for working toward developing positive relationships with all parents is so that all children will succeed. Therefore, even if we are not concerned with appearing to be overly strong or confident, we ought to at least be concerned with maintaining positive and productive conversations with parents. A difficult parent who arrives at the school feeling angry is not a parent we can speak with in a rational, productive manner. If we must employ some well-planned techniques to calm this parent down and "get down to business," then we are certainly behaving in a manner that brings us closer to the achievement of our goal—namely, positive and productive relationships with parents for their children's benefit.

Finally, consider the benefits that these communication methods can bring you in terms of how the rest of the school community perceives you. Because teachers play such important roles in the lives of a community's children, they always should appear confident and in control. Although it is never imperative that teachers appear to know all the answers, it is always important that students, colleagues, parents, and all other school stakeholders know that teachers are confident in their abilities. Intimidating parents, angry because of a one-sided story they may have heard from their child, enter all teachers' classrooms from time to time. It's actually inevitable. It is so important to your success with these relationships that you not let parents believe that you are ever frightened, uneasy, or intimidated.

Again, it really doesn't matter what your position is in a school. If difficult parents are able to intimidate you, not only do you risk losing the respect of those around you, but also you increase the odds that you will cave in to the difficult parents and yield to their requests. Other parents who see this happen may become confused or upset and think that bullying and intimidating you are ways to get what they want. The squeaky wheel should

If difficult parents are able to intimidate you, not only do you risk losing the respect of those around you, but also you increase the odds that you will cave in to the difficult parents and yield to their requests.

not always get the grease. It's not only important that difficult parents don't see you sweat, but that parents watching from the outside don't either.

The techniques and behaviors discussed in this chapter remain just as effective regardless of what grade or subject you teach. All schools have difficult parents to contend with. All teachers need a certain degree of assistance in learning how always to appear confident and in control. We are certain most readers will agree that teachers encounter their share of difficult parents who arrive at the classroom door angry and unannounced. Even if the teacher is right and the parent misunderstands an issue that may have arisen at school, the teacher is apt to get nervous when the parent storms into the classroom screaming. Remembering the methods described in this chapter will not automatically lead to a peaceful conversation filled with mutual growth and understanding, but it will accomplish one important step toward this noble goal. It will make it so that you never let 'em see you sweat. As we all know from experience, this is half of the battle.

10

What If the Parent Is Right?

One of the greatest difficulties educators encounter is when a parent calls to complain about our alleged inappropriate behavior, and it turns out that the parent is right. These situations do not necessarily need to involve allegations of gross misconduct on our part. Instead, they can be simple situations like a miscalculated grade or a misplaced student assignment. The reason for the difficulty has little to do with the error that was made. It has a great deal to do however, with the challenge of not losing our self-worth or being defensive while acknowledging that the parent's complaint has merit.

When parents call, email, or make a surprise visit to the classroom to report their perception of a problem, more often than not they are missing some facts. As a result, the perception they arrived at is often misguided. Sometimes, however, they are right. Sometimes, the wrong that the parents perceive to have occurred actually did occur. In these difficult times, what's an educator to do?

Again, although the scope of the issue may be different if you are an administrator than if you are a teacher, the approaches for responding to these parents are very similar. Though it sounds so simple and clichéd, honesty is always the

In dealing with difficult parents, you should never feel the need to always be right. . . . It should never be about winning or losing. It should be about arriving at a common understanding and doing so in an agreeable, productive manner.

best policy. In dealing with difficult parents, you should never feel the need to always be right. Never believe that your teaching skills or educational qualifications hinge, even to a slight degree, on showing difficult parents that their perception of a situation is incorrect. It should never be about winning or losing. It should be about arriving at a common understanding and doing so in an agreeable, productive manner.

Whether thinking back to my days as a teacher or to those I spent as a principal, I always remained mindful of the fact that my interactions with difficult parents were designed to get us both on the proverbial same page. Perhaps more significantly, I really wanted to get us there in an agreeable manner with the hope that it would lessen any future difficulties. It was perfectly okay for the parents to be right. In fact, I was quick to point out how much I appreciated the parents' ability to uncover the facts about issues and to present them to me in a way that would expedite the correction of any wrongdoing. The key in all of these situations was to appreciate the parents for bringing issues to my attention and to quickly inform them that the wrong that was committed was not done so intentionally. Then, in all cases, I made sure that I affirmed the parents for presenting the issue in a rational, understanding manner, even if that was not at all the manner in which they actually presented it. Consider this example as an illustration:

The Incorrect Grade

All teachers, whether they use electronic grading systems or hand calculations, run the risk of making the occasional grading error. While these errors are often insignificant, and while we all have no problem acknowledging and then correcting them, they can send the already difficult parents into a fit. No sooner does the student bring the paper that has been incorrectly scored home, then the parents contact us or arrive at the classroom demanding that justice be served. As discussed in the previous chapter, it is important that the angry parents not see you sweat. Employing the techniques from Chapter 7, you should welcome the parents into the room. Acknowledge their feelings with a comment like, "Gee, Mrs. Jones, you seem so upset. Please come in so I can help you with your problem." Then let them explain the error. At this point, you have shown the parents that you are not defensive, you have left open the door that maybe they are correct, and your professional responses have subtly pointed out that the parents' behavior is not at present as rational as yours.

It is wise and prudent to look next at the grade in question and determine if, in fact, you made an error. Assuming it was, you should thank the parents for pointing it out, quickly correct it, and close with a comment like, "Caring parents like you are exactly what our schools need more of. Thank you for pointing this out to me so that I could correct it. Your cooperative nature is exactly what will help us work as a team for the benefit of your child." In doing so, you have lost no dignity, you have shown the parents that you are human and, consequently, make mistakes, and you have illustrated for them how agreeably such issues can be resolved.

"Sorry" Seems to Be the Hardest Word

There is one more very significant step that you should employ when a parent is right. If the parent is upset about something that you have done wrong, you should apologize. The same is true whether you did something wrong, or if the complaint is about somebody else on the staff. By apologizing, particularly in the cases where the issue involves something somebody else did, you are not necessarily admitting any guilt or acknowledging a wrongdoing on anyone's part. You don't have to be sorry that a staff member did something that a parent alleges he or she did. You can simply be sorry that the parent perceives that the event happened and is upset about it.

If the error is yours, at the end of the conversation be secure enough to apologize again. When parents recognize that you

When parents recognize that you are sorry when you do things incorrectly, it is amazing how willing they become to forgive you. When you refuse to ever acknowledge that you, or anybody else in your school, is capable of doing wrong, then many parents go on a mission to prove just how wrong you actually are.

are sorry when you do things incorrectly, it is amazing how willing they become to forgive you. When you refuse to ever acknowledge that you, or anybody else in your school, is capable of doing wrong, then many parents go on a mission to prove just how wrong you actually are. The importance of saying that you are sorry is explored in even greater depth in Chapter 11.

Sometimes It's Important to Be First

If you make a mistake that could lead to parents becoming upset and calling you to complain, call the parents first. Though we may initially dread the idea and fear that we are going to receive an earful, the pain this saves in the long run can be tremendous. In all times of discomfort, it is usually a good idea to be proactive. By contacting parents who you know are upset before they contact you, a great deal of their anger can be defused. If, instead, we hide our heads in the sand and hope that the parents won't call us, then nine times out of ten all we do is give the parents more time to become even angrier.

I can recall one time several years ago when I was in a terrible hurry (as I usually am), and I stopped to pick up a dry cleaning order on the way home. I pulled into the parking lot where the dry cleaner was located and bolted from my car to pick up my order. The clerk who greeted me was very pleasant, handed me several items on hangers, took my money, and wished me a good day. Grabbing the hangers, I hurried to my car and headed home. When I got home and was putting the clothing in my closet, I noticed that one of my shirts was missing. My immediate thought was, "That stupid clerk! How could he forget to give me all of my clothes? I'll bet he remembered to charge me for everything, though!"

As I walked toward the telephone to call and complain, reading the receipt on the way, I noticed that the red light on the answering machine was lit, indicating that I had received a message. I pressed the "play" button and was surprised to hear, "Hi, this is Jason from Crown Dry Cleaners. Look, I'm really sorry, but I forgot to give you one of the shirts you had paid for. It's no excuse, but we had been so busy today that I must have mixed it up with an incoming order. For your trouble and because we really appreciate your business, the manager has authorized me to offer to clean your next five shirts for free. You can pick this one up at your convenience. Again, I'm really sorry." Do you know how I felt after listening to that? I felt pretty stupid, to tell you the truth. After all, everybody makes mistakes. I was embarrassed that I even got angry in the first place.

Think of how differently this all might have turned out if Jason had not called me. I would have called him, probably behaving in a manner that I would later be ashamed of. Maybe he would have become defensive, and the outcome would have been entirely different. At best, he would have let me blow off steam, but made the same offer to clean the next five shirts for free. Then, I would have felt guilty for acting the way I did, and both of us would have had a bad day. Because he proactively acknowledged his simple mistake, though, this story had a happy ending.

This same concept can be applied to our dealings with parents. Sometimes, we do make mistakes. Sometimes, particularly with the difficult ones, the parents become angry. In all cases, we gain nothing by becoming defensive and insisting that we did nothing wrong. When we are honest, when we admit our mistakes, when we apologize for the trouble they may have caused, and when we are proactive, then a parent who is right gives us the opportunity to be right also.

11

The Best Way to Get in the Last Word . . .

There is an old saying that the best way to get in the last word is to apologize. This saying may be true in a great number of settings, but it may be most applicable and effective in working with difficult parents. We have found that the single best defuser in any situation is the apology. Many educators do this. However, the specific wording that we use is essential because it can allow us to calm the waters and yet retain our dignity. It is very difficult to say, "I was wrong . . ." It is even more difficult to say that when it is not true. But there is one way we can approach all situations that will help satisfy even the most aggressive parents while at the same time allowing us to be honest in our approach. Let's take a look at this method.

I Am Sorry That Happened

It is amazing how one approach can apply to a myriad of situations, whether the situation is between an educator and a student, between two teachers, an administrator-teacher struggle, or any challenging situation involving a parent. Being able to say, "I am sorry that happened," is universally applicable language. Imagine the following scenario (though it probably will not take much imagining!).

You receive a phone call at night from an irate parent who is a consistent pain in the neck (or even lower). The parent belligerently exclaims that his or her son, David, was being picked on in the hallway (or at recess, in the locker room, etc.) at school that day, and nobody did anything about it. You ask the parent to share a little more information, and the parent continues to share details that apparently a couple of other boys shoved David against the wall and were threatening him and calling him names. Obviously, you know little more about the situation than what the parent has just shared with you. However, you can rely on your apology wording.

You can say, "Mrs. Smith, I am sorry that happened. I appreciate you calling to share this information, and I will make sure I look into it tomorrow, and I will also visit with David to see if he has any more details to share. I will also make sure that I visit with the other boys that were involved, but I sure am sorry that happened."

Examine closely what you said. You did not assume any responsibility for the incident, but you still expressed that you were sorry it happened. You might be thinking to yourself right now, "I am not sorry that it happened; that is a lie." Well, not if you add a second part to the statement. With the rudest and most unpleasant parents to work with, I say verbally, "I am sure sorry that happened." However, *to myself* I add, ". . . otherwise I wouldn't be visiting with you right now!" And that is the truth. With our most challenging parents, we would schedule a root canal in lieu of meeting with them if we could.

And, truth be told, regardless of what occurred, now that you have to spend even more time dealing with them, aren't you truly sorry that it happened? This perspective was amazingly refreshing to me and allowed me to help them feel that I was seeing things from their point of view while allowing me to retain my dignity in the situation.

It is also essential to make sure that we use a sympathetic tone and manner. As in all settings, if we allow rudeness, arrogance, impatience, or sarcasm to

> **If we allow rudeness, arrogance, impatience, or sarcasm to drip into our voice, then we have generally fanned the flames in a very negative way.**

drip into our voice, then we have generally fanned the flames in a very negative way.

This exact same approach is appropriate in a face-to-face setting. If parents march into your classroom or office and share any situation that is of concern to them regarding their child, stating that you are sorry that it happened may be very beneficial. This is also a productive approach for a principal defending a teacher. You are not blaming staff members, or necessarily defending them, but you are truly sorry that the situation occurred. Getting parents calmed down and into a listening mode is an important step toward developing an amicable solution to their concerns.

Getting parents calmed down and into a listening mode is an important step toward developing an amicable solution to their concerns.

Even if you initiate the conversation, this same tool is appropriate. If you have to call parents and tell them that their daughter was cheating on a test or is being held after school, regardless of the circumstance, you are really sorry that it happened. This attitude also helps develop some common ground with parents. Because, regardless of their disposition, they are probably sorry that it happened, also. And in any type of negotiation, establishing some commonalities is an important step to settling the issue in a way that both sides can live with.

An Ear, Not an Answer

Often, even irate parents want someone to listen to them more than they want someone to solve their problems. They may live in an environment where they feel no one listens. Their work may

Often, even irate parents want someone to listen to them more than they want someone to solve their problems.

not be of a structure that allows them to share their feelings, perspectives, or thoughts. And honestly, with many of the most challenging parents that we work with, their children probably don't listen too well to them either. Thus, if we can help them feel that we are on their side and that we are attempting to see things from their point of view, it may go a long way to calming them down and building up a level of trust with them that may serve us well in the future.

Sharing with people, "I am sorry that happened," can help us achieve many of these goals, and it is just as appropriate to say to the nicest parents in the school as to the ones that we least look forward to working with. Practicing this language in many situations outside as well as inside school can help us to use it effectively during more stressful or confrontational settings involving parents.

12

Do You Feel Defensive? If So, Something Is Wrong

One of our favorite sayings is that educators should never be defensive, *and* they should never be offensive. If we are truly caring people, then as teachers, principals, and superintendents, we should never be defensive when we deal with parents. We might feel awkward, uncomfortable, intimidated, but we should not feel *defensive*. If we are making all of our decisions based on what is best for students, then this defensiveness should not be occurring. If we do feel defensive, then it is probably because we, or someone we are attempting to support, has done something wrong.

If we are wrong, then it is essential that we apologize for our errors and then work diligently to not have that incident occur again. In this chapter, we discuss the situation in which the parent is wrong and we are right. However, being in touch with our feelings can help us to correct things before we put ourselves in the position of having to defend our actions. Let's take a look at a couple of examples.

> *Being in touch with our feelings can help us to correct things before we put ourselves in the position of having to defend our actions.*

Rules That Make No Sense

We truly believe that you do not control anyone's behavior by rules. We believe that everyone knows what the "rules" in life are and attempting to change inappropriate behaviors through rules makes no sense. It is sort of like feeling the need to post a *No Smoking!* sign in the bathroom at school. Believe me, they all know they should not be smoking; it is just that the irresponsible students choose to do it anyhow. It is sort of like posting a *Shoplifters Will Be Prosecuted!* sign in a store. Trust me, the people who might shoplift know it is wrong—that is why they make sure no one is looking.

Well, in education, sometimes we do these same things. We attempt to hide behind rules. I was as guilty as anyone. I remember my first year as a seventh grade math teacher. I did not want to have to mess with students turning in assignments late, leaving class to go to their lockers, and so forth. And for my own personal convenience, I did not want to have to grade late papers anyhow.

So I decided to have a rule that if you did not have your assignment with you in class, you would receive a zero on it. Boy, that made sense to me. As a matter of fact, for about the first third of the year it seemed to be a pretty good rule. Not too many students forgot their work and the ones that did were fairly irresponsible ones who probably did poorly on the assignment anyway. Realistically, most of the students who forgot their work weren't going to be competing for valedictorian anyhow.

I could also rationalize this rule by thinking that I was teaching responsibility to irresponsible seventh grade students. And I gave enough different assignments that generally missing any one homework grade probably wasn't too significant in terms of a grade. But then something happened. One of the nicest girls in the class, a hyper-responsible, straight-A student, forgot the most important assignment of the year. Not only was this a major assignment, but it was large enough that it would reduce her quarter grade dramatically and even impact her semester grade. Yikes! She had it done, but in a hurry to not be late to class (she also had perfect attendance as well as no tardies for the year), she left her work in her locker. To make matters even worse, her locker was just outside the door of the classroom.

Well, I can guarantee you that if I gave her a zero and her parents called me out of concern I would have felt very defensive. And the reason? The reason I would have felt defensive was because it was a silly rule to begin with. The impact, by chance, on this one student was so much greater than the impact on others who had missed minor assignments. When I realized how defensive I felt, I knew I had to change the rule and make amends with previous students who I had wronged.

Though it is nice to teach students lessons in responsibility, I guess maybe it is even more important to teach them lessons in empathy.

You Can't Make Sense Out of No Sense

Another example of being in touch with your feelings occurred when I was a first-year varsity basketball coach. We were having practice over the week between Christmas and New Year's Day. The day after Christmas, we had practice, and two of my players were not there. They had not let me know they would be absent. They were just skipping practice. So I did the all too common thing. I punished the players who were there by having them run dozens of extra sprints. This is a traditional approach still used by some coaches. The purpose of this idea is to cause those angry players who were there and were disciplined to in turn "punish" the guilty absent players. They feel that this type of peer pressure is one way to get others to alter their behaviors.

You know what? You don't have to be a genius to know that there is something wrong with this approach. Though I miraculously did not hear from any parents, I still realized that this was a silly thing to do. The only reason I did it is because that is what other coaches had done. I guess the other lesson that I would have taught the team was that if you hear of a player who is going to skip practice, you had better go ahead and skip practice, too!

This same thing happens all too often in classrooms also. Requiring all students to put their heads on their desks for five

Punishing or even sternly lecturing an entire class because a few students misbehaved does little to establish credibility with either students or parents.

minutes because two students were talking does not make any sense. Punishing or even sternly lecturing an entire class because a few students misbehaved does little to establish credibility with either students or parents.

Being sensitive to these inappropriate approaches can allow us as educators to avoid or minimize situations in which we have strong feelings of defensiveness. Just being aware of our emotions and being in touch with them can help us to establish reasonable guides and expectations for student behavior.

Why Didn't I Know?

Being in touch with these defensive feelings is applicable to all educators when we fail to contact parents with information that is important. This is especially true if it is a situation we may have to deal with at a later point. If we get involved earlier, there may be less baggage or pent up emotions that would prevent us from being as productive as we would like. A common scenario is when we have to call parents over minor offenses that have reached their limit. Here is an example:

As principals, if a teacher regularly sends students to the office with a note that says, "This is the fifth time in the last two weeks Jimmy has come to class without a pencil," we will probably make an initial effort to support this staff member. We may decide to punish this student, call the parent, and share the consequences. If we call the student's mother and share with her that her son is being given detention because this is the fifth time he has come to class without a pencil we are likely to get this reaction from his mom: "Why didn't I know?"

As principals, we feel defensive because we realize that the mother is right. A rule of thumb we have for all educators applies equally to people in more formal educational leadership roles. That is, that we should never feel defensive. If we do, it may be because we or someone in our school is doing something wrong. In this case, the teacher was doing something inappropriate, so we felt defensive when we were attempting to support her.

Asking and expecting staff to contact the parent *before* the student is sent to the office is an appropriate guideline. Realizing that some of the teachers may not regularly contact parents, providing them with some role modeling may be very appropriate. Explain that the call from the teacher is more effective because it is asking for the parent's assistance, not setting up a negative first contact regarding a punishment. The teacher could contact the parent and say, "Mrs. Johnson, I was wondering if I could get your help with something? Jimmy has not brought a pencil to class three times in the last week. I was not sure if you were aware of this, but I wanted to request your assistance before he ends up falling behind in class or before the office has to get involved. Could I get your help in visiting with him and making sure that he leaves for school prepared? Your assistance would greatly be appreciated."

Few parents would not agree to help. If the first contact is made in the form of a request for assistance, prior to their son or daughter being in "trouble," this is a relationship-building contact. Now, we realize that a few parents will not follow through, and at some point, the office may be involved. However, the difference is, at that time, rather than the principal feeling defensive because the parents "did not know," the parents will be the ones feeling on the spot because they did not follow through on their word. The point is not to make the parents feel defensive, but to make sure the educators are not backpedaling. Once this expectation is established, the teachers who do make this initial contact will end up preventing many office referrals.

This same scenario applies equally to all classroom teachers. If the first contact with parents can be to call and ask for their help, we may be able to avoid situations where parents ask us why they did not know earlier and then we feel the need to defend our actions. Instead, using a proactive interaction allows the parents and us to be on the same side. Consider this when you share with the parent that you do not want Jimmy to fall behind in his work; does the parent want Jimmy to fall behind? Of course not. When you share that you do not want to have to get the office involved, do Jimmy's parents want to get the office involved? Of course not. And keep in mind, the more belligerent the parents are, often the less they trust authority. In these cases, they really do not want to get the office involved! Thus, your relationship has started out on a positive note involving things that you and they agree on.

Taking time to reflect on our feelings can help us to be more effective in developing guidelines and expectations that are appropriate for our students, classrooms, and schools. Understanding the long-range benefit of dramatically reducing the frequency with which we feel that we are behind the eight ball can allow us to view our jobs and our contact with parents in a more positive and productive light.

Part IV

Dealing with Parents in Difficult Situations

13

Delivering Bad News

It is never any fun to be the bearer of bad news. Few of us ever look forward to ruining someone's day or potentially having to deal with the emotion of the recipient's reaction. As educators, some of us may be a little hesitant simply because of past experiences we have had or because of negative situations others may have described for us. Additionally, we may have to contact or work with a parent who has a less than favorable reputation and that may add to our trepidation. In this chapter, we will focus on methods, tips, language, and approaches that can help us to most successfully tread these troubled waters.

The Worse the News, the More Effort We Use

Sometimes we have to deliver bad news when the parent contacts us or catches us unprepared. Many of the techniques we describe in this chapter and others in this section are very appropriate in all circumstances, including a parent-initiated contact. But typically, the ball is in our court in terms of having to initiate that contact in some fashion. One of the first standards we should establish is that *the worse the news, the more thought and effort*

> *One of the first standards we should establish is that the worse the news, the more thought and effort we need to put into delivering it.*

we need to put into delivering it. As difficult as it may be, it is very important that we make personal contact when we have negative news to share with a parent. And the more challenging the parent is, the more effort we must put forward.

It is essential that we seldom, if ever, deliver bad news in writing. Most of the time if we email a parent or send notes home with students it is for our convenience or because it is easier for us in the short term than having to deal with a parent on the phone or in person. We know that a certain percentage of parents may not have home phones, but generally, we should always make personal contact when delivering bad news.

One reason for this is very selfish. If you send a note home to difficult parents, your level of concern remains. You are not sure if they will be upset. If they are, you may even imagine them showing up at your classroom or office unannounced in a fit of rage. Thus, potentially your level of discomfort may continue indefinitely. Also, if they do call or drop in unexpectedly, you may be less prepared for them than if you were in charge of the contact. The final reason, and we will discuss this further in this chapter, is that if students carry notes home, they get to share their point of view with the parents before you do. Even if the note is mailed or delivered in a hermetically sealed envelope, they will still get to share their side of the story before you do. And especially if it involves some type of misbehavior on their part, there is a *slight* chance that their version may be different than yours. With our most challenging students and their difficult parents, the kids usually know how to push the parents' buttons. If they didn't, then the student would generally not be so challenging.

The Phone Is Our Best Friend . . .

Unless It Is Ringing

Probably the most effective and convenient way to contact a parent with bad news is using the phone. We always want to contact the parents if at all possible *before* the student has a chance to visit with them. This is especially true with the most difficult of parents in discipline situations or other times when the student has done something wrong. If students share their story first, then often we are in a defensive mode when we finally do reach the parents. They already have a viewpoint, and now we have to work to alter it. Now, we are very aware that many of our parents know of their child's willingness to bend the truth. However, this book is focused on dealing with our *most difficult* parents and difficult situations. These situations may be the ones in which we can rely on the student's honesty the least.

We need to develop a consistent approach when contacting any parent for any reason. Each phone call, whether it be for a positive stroke or discussing a troubling situation should start out the same. We do not want parents to develop a negative mindset simply because of our first words or tone. Thus, you should develop a structure that you start all calls with. If you will recall the wording for the positive phone calls discussed in Chapter 6, you will notice that every parent contact would start in the same manner. Additionally, we need to use the same level, relaxed, and confident voice in all situations. Again, if we can practice our parent contacts by delivering good news, it can help us refine the specific wording and tone that we want to use in all phone conversations with family members. Here is an example of a potential script for delivering bad news:

> Hi, Mrs. Johnson, this is Tom Walker, Kenny's math teacher at Smith Junior High. I am sorry to bother you at work (or home, depending on where you called), but today Kenny tripped a girl in class and as a result he will receive two hours detention.

If you did not contact the parent before the student did, you could also add something to the effect of:

> Hi, Mrs. Johnson, this is Tom Walker, Kenny's math teacher at Smith Junior High. I am sorry to bother you at work (or home, depending on where you called). I do not know if Kenny shared this with you or not, but today Kenny tripped a girl in class and as a result he will receive two hours detention.

By doing this, you could gather information on what the student told his or her parent. Additionally, you always want to shift the focus of the conversation to the future. Regardless of whether the student, parent, and you agree on what happened or the consequences, we all want to make sure it does not happen again. Chapter 16 provides great detail on language and ways to help shift to a future focus. This is especially valuable in delivering bad news. Additionally, Chapter 14 helps us develop a way to get the parent to support our decision, and Chapter 15 provides some tools if they say we are not being fair.

He Never Lies to Us!

It is amazing how many parents will respond to a difference between the student's story and the teacher version by saying, "My child never lies to me!"

Again, as professional educators, we do not ever argue. Parents who respond like that are likely to be ready to argue. Instead of settling in for a negative discussion, treat them as though they were telling the truth and bring up a past inappropriate behavior by the student. In other words, assume the child does tell their parent everything. This can allow a shift away from the disputed incident and put you more in control of the situation. Rather than getting into a detailed discussion about whether or not it was really Jimmy talking in class inappropriately today, you could respond, without using sarcasm (though we know it will be tempting) by saying:

> It sounds like you all have a very rare and special relationship. The fact that he never, ever lies to you is a tribute to both of you. Mrs. Smith, what did you think when Jimmy shared with you that he had to have his seat changed in the classroom *last Monday* because of throwing paper?

Often this will accomplish two goals. One is that it will at least temporarily move the conversation from a point that the parents dispute and feel very empowered to argue about to one that they might not have any knowledge of. It also tempers their insistence that "my son tells me everything." If you do this in a very professional and calm manner, you can typically move the parents back to the issue at hand. Assuming that their child does not really disclose everything to them, they may be in more of a mindset to be reasonable.

Prior to even responding to the parent, a first line of defense may be to ignore their comment to see if it goes away. We want to see if their argument is a "deal breaker." For example, sometimes challenging people just throw stuff at a wall (or at you) to see if it sticks. They may rattle off attack after attack. They could accuse the teacher of being unfair, of picking on their child, of not liking boys, etc. Rather than feeling the need to counter each point, ignore them and see if they go away.

> *Sometimes challenging people just throw stuff at a wall (or at you) to see if it sticks. They may rattle off attack after attack. . . . Rather than feeling the need to counter each point, ignore them and see if they go away.*

If a parent accuses you of being unfair and you do not respond to the accusation but rather continue in a professional manner, and the parent does not bring it up again, then it is not a deal breaker. However, if you respond, it is actually likely to accelerate the parent's tone or be something that the parent will keep going back to because they sense that it "got to you." This may just seem childish, because it really is childish. Some people are 30 going on 13 and they fall back into an adolescent mode of name-calling. When someone responds to the action, it makes it more likely that the person will repeat the action. If your first response can be a professional and self-controlled ignoring, then often times it will go away. Here is another way to handle the, "My child never lies to me!" scenario. However, it requires even more self-control on your part and mandates that there is no hint of sarcasm.

If parents say, "My child never lies to me!" ignore them. If they don't bring it up again, then they were just using it as a weapon. If they keep repeating it, gently and sensitively say this:

> What you and your child share is a very special relationship. It is something I hope to develop with my own children. I would love to hear more about how you were able to build that special bond. We have

so many families here who could benefit from your guidance. There has been some discussion of having a series of parent workshops in our district. Would you mind if I passed along your name as someone they might want to contact to help all of us learn how to improve our parenting skills?

Now, you cannot have the least bit of smirk or arrogant tone when you do this. If you are not 100 percent sure about your ability to manage yourself, do not even try it. However, this parent has never had anyone act as if they believe them before. If you can pull this off, they will never take this approach with you again. They will either feel validated for the first time in their lives or drop it because they realize that they have been discovered as a fraud.

Your Honor, I Object

Though some of our challenging parents (and students) will want to act like lawyers, keep in mind that when we contact the family members we want to limit the amount of detail that we go into. This is doubly true with the people who will most want to pick apart every single action we took while attempting to avoid any focus on the actions of their child. This may not be easy to accomplish, but again shifting the focus to the future can help with this. To center on the future, you can say, for example, "Mrs. Jones what do you think we can do to help avoid this type of situation in the future?" or "Mr. Smith would you please visit with Jennifer tonight and discuss alternative behaviors that she could choose in the future?"

This language helps us to avoid a CSI-like recreation of the events. It also helps empower parents by giving them something to center on that they can control. And finally, it helps us to focus on the one thing that we all agree on, and that is that we do not want this to occur in the future.

Be Aware of What You Don't Know

When I was an assistant principal dealing with discipline, many times I found myself talking with parents about issues that I did not observe firsthand. Regardless, I still had to figure out a way to work effectively with the situation. One way that worked was to be honest with the parent. I would often say, "One of the tough things about this situation, Mr. Martinez, is that for the two people talking right now, neither one of us was there." This would allow me to focus on what we did have control over. We could then center on the "what can we do to make sure this does not occur again" conversation.

If the parents were very belligerent, then I would shift the conversation to something that I did know about. For example, if parents insisted that someone was picking on their son and that their child was wrongly being accused, I would steer the dialogue from something I did not have firsthand knowledge of to something that I *did* have personal awareness of. The conversation may take a turn in this direction:

> One of the tough things about this situation, Mr. Martinez, is that neither one of us was there. And obviously, neither one of us can sort out exactly what did occur. However, I want to share with you what I saw your son do last Wednesday. I saw him in the cafeteria disturbing other students, throwing trash on the floor, and poking three students. Now I took care of his behavior that day by having him help pick up trash in the cafeteria. Neither of us saw what happened today, but I almost contacted you last week over what I did see. And if today he interacted with other students like he did last week I could imagine that his behavior would have caused the situation to escalate.

What I was doing with this conversation was reestablishing control of the discussion. Rather than focusing on something that I did not have firsthand knowledge about (today's behavior), I centered on something that I did observe that was inappropriate. Not only did this take the focus off of this disputed situation, it also defended the teacher by indicating that she was more tolerant and fair than I would have been.

Again, you need to be selective in using this approach, but in very challenging situations this is a powerful tool. The same thing can occur with other students accusing a child of bullying.

Your contact with parents this time may be about a reported rather than observed behavior. However, if the parents choose to be uncooperative, you might be able to gain control of the situation by referring to a bullying situation that you did observe involving the same student, but that the bullying victim did not report. Thus, the latest one must have been even worse for the student (victim) to come to you to complain this time. Not only will this type of approach generally put you in control of the discussion, it may give you a little bit of a confidence boost and help you gain some more control of your emotions.

But This Is a Really Tough Class

In any type of service occupation, we have to work in situations that may not be totally within our control. If we work at a store in the complaint department, we are probably not responsible for the faulty merchandise that the customers are complaining to us about. However, to the customers who ordered it, that is irrelevant. They do not have much concern about your perspective; they primarily care about what they want. The same thing is true with parents. For the most part, they only care about their child. We are not saying this with any criticism. The parents who truly care about their children are often the least of our concerns. It is the parents who do not care about the children who create the most challenging situations.

We need to make sure that we accept responsibility for the situation and not pass the buck. It may be a challenging class, possibly your most challenging ever, but that does not matter to the parents. Their primary concern is how their child is doing.

With this in mind, we need to make sure that we accept responsibility for the situation and not pass the buck. It may be a challenging class, possibly your most challenging ever, but that does not matter to the parents. Their primary concern is how *their* child is doing.

If the most effective teachers in a school give a test or homework assignment and the students do poorly on it—and this can happen to the best of us—who do those teachers blame? Themselves. They feel that they should have explained it better or provided more guidance practice before they gave the assignment. And the real question is, who is the one person's behavior in that class they can control? Their own, of course.

If the least effective teacher in a school gives a test or homework assignment and the students do poorly on it, who do they blame? The students, last year's teacher, or maybe the parents.

The point of this is that trying to pass off responsibility to someone that we or the parents cannot control is a very temporary situation. It will only lead to greater frustration. In addition to shifting the responsibility away from us, it also shifts responsibility away from the parents and students. In actuality, that is where we want the responsibility focused.

Similar to complaining to a teacher or a principal about something in the school, the people who are sharing their concern with the complaint department do not care who is at fault, they just want the problem solved. Parents do not care if this is a difficult class with challenging students. That is not a justification for their child not receiving appropriate attention. All these excuses really do is tell them that you are not effective in working with their child. It does not help with personal credibility.

What If They Tell Us Not to Call Them at Work?

Often the parents we have to tell bad news to are the same parents we have to contact on a frequent basis. Sometimes we should give them a number on our speed-dialing list. If we attempt to call these people at work, sometimes they will tell us that we cannot because they might get in trouble or even lose their jobs. For the average parent or an even mildly cooperative parent, I would work hard to comply. However, if I have a very disruptive student for which nothing seems to be working, or tremendously uncooperative parents, I will make it a point to contact the parents at work. I will still always be nice and professional; however, if that is what it takes to get their attention or to motivate them to assist with the needs of their children, then I feel empowered and maybe even obligated to try every option that I have. It is important they become aware that the way to get me to stop calling them at work is for them to positively alter their child's behavior.

By the same token, if I am supposed to call the mom, and when I do, I hear from an angry dad the next day, I will often switch and instead call the dad. Though he may be the most offensive party to work with, I might as well deal with him under my initiative rather than under his. And hopefully, I will also be down to just one phone call rather than two.

Despite our preparation and very best efforts, sometimes when we deliver less than positive news, the conversation can get heated. Being able to defuse the situation is critical. Several other chapters provide additional strategies and solutions for you, but we'd like to share one of our favorites now.

Please Don't Talk to Me Like That

We do believe it is important to allow people to let off a little steam. We all feel frustrated at times, and sometimes that is all it takes for someone to calm down. However, sometimes the tirade continues a little too long or becomes too ugly. What can we do? The single best method we have ever used we call "please don't talk to me like that." Again, like all communications, the style and approach we use will greatly determine its effectiveness. Let's take a look at the specific language involved.

If the parents have pushed your tolerance to the limit or they are being inappropriately personal or rude, here is how you could respond. Keep in mind the tone you use would be very calm, you would talk s-l-o-w-l-y and gently, but you would want to have a quiet confidence in your voice. What you would say is:

> Mrs. Smith, please don't talk to me like that. I will *never* speak to you like that, and I will *never* speak to your child like that, so please don't talk to me like that.

Realize that this is not a threat and it is not an order. Nobody likes to be told what to do, especially someone who is already angry. However, it does accomplish two things. It is a very reasonable and professional request, and it is a promise regarding how we will treat you and how we will treat your son or daughter. This is a very calming dialogue if we handle it in the correct manner. We try not to interrupt the other person at the beginning, but if it is past that point, we might. However, the more heated the other party is, the slower and calmer we force ourselves to be. Another important thing about the wording on the previous page is that it is not inflammatory language. We did not want to ever incite an upset person.

Now realize that we also made a commitment ourselves regarding how we will treat those parents and their child. Of course, that should not be a problem, because in order to deal with a difficult parent we first must be able to deal with ourselves!

Little Pitchers Have Big Ears

There is an old saying that "little pitchers have big ears." What this means is that as adults, if we ever say anything we do not want children to repeat, then we had better make sure they do not hear us. This is critical in educator/parent communications. We will allow parents to vent for a while. However, we will not allow them to act inappropriately with the student present. We are happy to meet with them and discuss their issue, and we have no secrets to keep from their children. But we will not allow them to role-model improper behavior toward an educator in front of their child. Using the dialogue given is one way to help if you are meeting in person. And obviously you can ask the child to step out of the room. However, if the parent calls you in the evening, you may not be as able to monitor who is present in the room.

And with our most challenging parents, often the student is there in the room with them egging them on. We do believe it is essential to attempt to prevent this from occurring. If you feel that the child is listening to inappropriate behavior on the part of the parent, you could say this to the parent:

I sure hope that there is no chance that Gregory can hear this conversation. I would be very disappointed if he could hear you talking to anyone in our school in this manner. I would never want him to get the impression that we can ever talk to someone in our school in that tone of voice, so I sure hope that is no chance Gregory can hear you speaking to me this way.

This may not always work, but it does two things. One is that it helps the parents understand that it is wrong for their son to be privy to this conversation. And the other is that it helps the parents get control of themselves and stop their inappropriate behavior.

Putting It All Together

There are many different approaches to delivering bad news to a parent. The first step is to decide what you want to say and how you want to say it. Another important facet is to develop as many resources and tools as you can to help you if the parent chooses not to respond in as appropriate a manner as you may wish. Also, keep in mind that as you develop your skills, sometimes we have to go into what is called the broken record mode and keep revisiting key points. Maybe four or five times in the conversation we have to refocus on the future by continuing to come back to, "Okay, Mrs. Smith, now what can we do to make sure that this behavior does not occur again?" Maintaining the proper focus can allow you to be in more control of yourself and as a result be in more control of the situation.

Always remember, also, that sometimes the parents who are most belligerent in defending their child are doing it out of guilt. They may be well aware that they have not been as attentive to the needs of their child as they should have been, so yelling at you is one way to show they care. Unfortunately for some of our most challenging parents, it may be the only way they have shown that they care.

14

But I Did Get a Good Deal

Examining the Car Salesperson

One experience that most of us have had is buying a car from a car dealership. Though we may cringe at the possibility of having to haggle when we go in, most people feel when they leave that they got a "good deal." To emphasize this point, I often present groups with the following scenario.

How many of you have bought a car from a car dealer over the last three years? In a group of 100 people, usually 80-plus percent of the hands go up. Then I ask, "How many of you think you got a good deal?" Almost as many hands go up. I then say, "Okay, now those of you who have not bought cars from dealers in the last three years, how many of you think that those people who raised their hands *really* got a good deal?" Amazingly, no hands go up. I then say, "Okay, those of you who have purchased a car, how many of you *really* think you got a good deal? How many of you think you really snookered that dealership?" Interestingly, very few people logically think they got a good deal, but emotionally many of us do. Even after going through this process, some people are still upset emotionally.

That shows the power of the car dealer. Even though logically we never get a "good deal," emotionally we feel that we do. Understanding this dynamic can be very beneficial in effectively interacting with parents, and anyone else for that matter. Several things happen. One of the most obvious when we look at it objectively, but potentially the most effective, is that the salesperson makes you *feel* that he or she is on your side. The other item to understand is that potentially in your mind, you are comparing the original or sticker price of the car to the final price that you actually paid. And since generally there is a fairly significant difference, you again feel that you got a good deal.

Or, the other situation could be that the price you received when you traded in your car was more than you were hoping to get, thus again leaving you feeling like you received a good deal on the car. Now, objectively we know that the sticker price was not really the price, and we are also aware that the price they gave us for our trade was actually just a discount off of the list price of the car we purchased; nonetheless, it makes us feel much more satisfied with the final outcome. My purpose in sharing this is not to have us debate whether or not you are a master negotiator. The point is to help you understand what effective negotiators do. What is even more ironic is that the more you want to argue that you did get a good deal, the more it probably proves the point that the dealer was successful in making you feel satisfied.

I want to share one more example to show the point of the dealmaker. For several years when I worked in a particular school district, I had the pleasure of transporting our opening session speakers to and from the airport. One year, I had to pick up a well-known gentlemen who had formerly been involved in professional sports. He did a nice job as a speaker, and I was taking him back to the airport. Making conversation, I asked him what he did now that he was out of sports. He said that he did negotiation seminars around the country. I commented that that must be very interesting. I then brought up my theory regarding car dealers. I asked him why he thought it was that everyone who buys a car thinks they got a good deal, and yet no one really gets a good deal. He laughed and agreed. Then he got very serious and sort of defiantly said, "You know in general that is true, but last month I bought a new car and I *did* get a good deal!"

That shows the emotional power of the car deal. A person who does negotiations for a living still is insistent that he got a good deal. Wow!

With that in mind, I always set out to make sure that people felt that they were treated fairly and with respect. However, in the toughest situations or in working with the most difficult people, I set an even higher standard. I actually wanted people to thank me when we were done visiting. As an assistant principal and principal, my goal was to have parents thank me when I suspended their son or daughter. That may sound like a lofty goal, but it is one that I feel that we can reach at least 90 percent of the time. Keep in mind that there is no more potentially adversarial relationship than working with car dealers. Trust me, they have the exact opposite interest than you have. Their goal is to make you spend as much money as possible, and your goal is to spend as little. If car dealers can make you feel like you got a good deal when they definitely do not have your best interests in mind, then educators can accomplish this same goal with parents. At least in education, both the parents and school personnel have the same interest in mind—doing what is best for the student. Let's take a look at how this concept can work.

Let Me Take Another Look Underneath That Hood

If as a teacher, you walk into a smoky student restroom in your school and there are two nervous students in there, it would be nice if you could approach them in a way in which they would admit they were smoking. If they denied they were doing anything wrong, then it would be very tough to resolve the situation. You did not really see them smoke, and even if you did, they might still choose to deny it. How could we best get them to come clean?

You could ask the students, "Do you all smoke in here every day or is this your first time?" Even sophisticated students are likely to respond, "It's our first time." You then treat them as if it is the first time they have smoked, they get suspended or whatever the consequences are, and you make sure their parents are aware that they admitted it. You even tell the students, "Since this is your first time and you admitted it, we'll only go with a three-day suspension." Even though the first occurrence always results in a three-day suspension, the students and parents are much more likely to be appreciative that they "got a good deal."

Imagine you teach fifth grade and you cannot get one of your students to admit they did something that other students told you occurred. You consistently ask them to admit it and they will not admit it. What should you do? You could say to them, "Can you at least reassure me that none of the first graders saw you do it? It would be terrible if any of the first graders saw you do it. Can you please reassure me of that?"

Then when the fifth grader sheepishly looks at you and assuredly says, "None of the first graders saw me do it. I promise none of the first graders saw me do it."

You now have the exact info you need. You contact their parents and say you have some good news and some bad news. "The bad news is your son is in trouble for . . . The good news is none of the first graders saw him do it. He assured me that none of the first graders saw him do it."

You can also add that since he admitted it all you are going to do is hold him in for recess for two days instead of a week. The student and parent both feel like they received a "good deal" and the relationships are still in tact.

Now, we realize that this is not always appropriate, and it should be used sparingly. However, when dealing with the most challenging of parents, it is always nice to keep a few things in reserve if needed. Gentler versions of this same approach can be very beneficial and used more frequently.

As a teacher, being able to say things like, "because she told the truth . . ." or "since it is the first week of school . . ." can be regular approaches that help people feel that they got off lighter than they might have otherwise. This approach can also be helpful to reinforce positive behaviors and approaches on the part of parents as well as students.

Though a person may spend $4 on gas to drive to another store to save $2.50, they still *feel* like it was a bargain. Keeping this in mind can help you approach parents in a way that will make them feel more supported.

Oftentimes as educators, we reduce negative consequences in our own mind before we share them with students or parents. We are a caring profession with sensitive people. In general, that is a positive. However, at times, being a little more manipulative may be of benefit.

Let's look at a fairly common situation of a student cheating on a quiz. We can react angrily and mentally decide that this student will flunk the quiz and be assigned three hours detention. However, before we share that with the student and parent we think to ourselves that she is generally a nice young lady, and it hasn't happened before, so we decide to tell the student that she will flunk the quiz and have to stay after school an hour. Then you call the parents that evening or before you have the opportunity, they call you angry that their daughter is being "double punished." First the F and then staying after school.

Then, you try to defend yourself by saying, "I should have given her three hours detention!" Next thing you know, you are in an argument, and you are really ticked off because in your mind you had already given the girl a break. Whatever the resolution to the situation finally is, both parties are upset. Even if you do not change your mind, you feel as though you gave in too much, and they are upset that you did not give in enough.

However, the approach could have been to tell the girl that she will receive an F on the quiz, and you are considering giving her three to five hours detention—you want to think about it for a while. Then, that evening after she has communicated with her parents the potential consequences, you call the parents and tell them how serious the situation is, but that you are also aware that she has not been in trouble before, so you are willing to adjust her punishment to an F and an hour detention. It is amazing how effective it is when you mention a more severe consequence, even fleetingly. The reduced punishment sounds so much better to the student and the parents.

I remember once that I wanted to get two cats. My wife was not too crazy about having a house pet of any kind. However, finally I got the nerve to ask if we could get three cats. She responded, "Three cats! No way can we get more than two cats." I hope she doesn't read this part of the book because until now she thinks she has gotten a pretty good deal.

Good for 90 Days or 3,000 Miles

Obviously, this approach is not applicable in every situation, and we have to use it judiciously in order for it to be effective. If every time you tried to buy cereal in a store you had to dicker for the actual price, this would get very old and annoying. Yet, doing it once in a while for a major purchase makes us feel special. Repeatedly or always taking this same approach will have diminishing or even negative returns.

However, remembering the basic concept of making people feel like they were treated fairly, or maybe even that they got a good deal, can go a long way in developing and maintaining positive relations. This is the type of approach that we can put in our bag of tricks and pull out when we have an especially challenging parent or an especially difficult situation. Understanding the concept and being aware of how it can apply to many situations can allow us to build a reserve of approaches that we can use during the most challenging times.

Making people feel like they were treated fairly, or maybe even that they got a good deal, can go a long way in developing and maintaining positive relations.

Applying It to the Classroom

A scenario that all classroom teachers dread, but many of us have faced, is when irate or obnoxious parents show up at your door and demand their child leave with them right now. Not only can this be intimidating to us, but it is horribly embarrassing for the student. Additionally, if the parents have not gone through the office, you may not even know if they are legally parents or guardians of the child. How do we handle this? Let's think of our automobile-hawking friend.

The real power of car salespeople is that they make the customers feel that they are on their side. Although they at worst really represent the car dealership, and at best, themselves, effective salespeople have the ability to make you feel that they are representing you.

Understand that many belligerent parents feel very resentful toward authority. They may not get along with their boss, they may have trouble with the law, and they may resent school people because of their past experiences. However, working to get on their side can be very beneficial.

My first year as a teacher, I was in a rural setting. One day when I was teaching, a man who appeared very intoxicated walked in the doorway of my class and loudly slurred, "I'm here to pick up Johnny. Let's go boy—now!" I was pretty confident he had not checked in at the office for a pass. I also had no idea what his relationship was with the student, and the alcohol smell he was emitting was an additional concern. The only thing I could think of was getting him away from the students and down to the office. Because my classroom did not have an intercom to call the office, I had few choices. And to be honest, if I am really concerned about a parent's stability, I would rather not dive for the intercom switch and raise his level of concern if I can help it anyhow. So I mentally put on my white shoes and slid into the sales mode.

I walked calmly toward the man and introduced myself. After very gingerly asking him if he had stopped by the office and getting brashly rebuked, I then shifted modes. I matched his demeanor and explained, "I am sorry to tell you, but you know the world nowadays. Nobody trusts honest people like you and me. We're always getting jacked around. Good guys like us are always gettin' hassled. So now, they make us go down to the office and check in. It sounds silly, but that's the deal we all have to fight. It would sure help me out if we could go down there. I'll show you where it is."

It was like this guy and I became best friends. We had the "world's against us" bond. He started saying things like, "damn right" and "good guys like us," but next thing you know we were heading down to the office. I caught another teacher's eye to watch my class, and we walked down to the office together just complaining about how the "world's fallin' apart." Another 10 minutes, and I could have sold him my late model Ford that had only been driven on Sundays.

15

What If They Use the "F" Word—Fair?

One challenge that every educator faces is when there is an accusation that something is not fair. Every teacher has a "classroom lawyer" who is constantly in the "It's not fair!" mode in life. As experienced teachers though, this may still become exasperating. We have often developed ways to reduce the amount of "fair debates" that occur in our classrooms. We may have established an effective approach that works with students; however, it is essential that we can also work with parents when they accuse us of not being fair with their child.

Though it is not an appropriate response in the classroom, a teacher may even be tempted to say something sarcastic like, "Well, life is not fair," or "This isn't a democracy!" As undesirable as this type of response is, it may at least work temporarily in the classroom with people much younger than us or with an imbalance of power, though it will probably eventually escalate into a more negative confrontation.

It reminds me of an old joke. A teacher sarcastically says to a student, "What do you think?" The student then snaps back, "Well, what do *you* think?" The teacher smugly drawls, "Well, I don't think . . . I know!" And the student quips a reply of, "Well, I don't think I know either!"

This type of interchange is unprofessional with students, and it is totally unacceptable with parents. With that in mind, how can we best respond to the parent who pulls out the "F" word on us—fair?

Be Fair, Be Square, or Be Both, Like Me

Obviously, one of the first things that we need to do in order to diminish the amount of "that's not fair" comments is to be fair. Not only, of course, to be fair, but to be perceived as being fair. Gary Phillips (1997) once said that, "Treating unequals equally is no justice." If we are working with people, especially young people, there are always going to be situations in which we cannot have a predetermined response. There are always going to be judgment calls. However, when we can have predetermined expectations and consequences and communicate them appropriately, it can help to reduce the "it's unfair" chanting. Of course, even these predetermined standards must be reasonable.

When we can have predetermined expectations and consequences and communicate them appropriately, it can help to reduce the "it's unfair" chanting.

I described in Chapter 12 my idea to give a zero to students who did not have their homework assignment with them at the beginning of class. If they left it in the locker, tough luck. As you may recall, this went fine for most of the first semester. Only a few students forgot their work, and they were primarily the lower-achieving students anyhow. Additionally, most of the assignments were routine homework that would not dramatically affect their grade to any significant degree.

Then, close to the end of the semester, one of the best and most responsible students in the class forgot a major assignment. It was left in her locker, which was just outside the classroom. It would significantly impact her grade for not only the quarter, but also the entire first semester. As I described in Chapter 12, I knew I was wrong and that ended my rule. And the only thing that I could do to be fair was let any of the students who had fallen prey to this ill-thought rule turn in their missing assignments. However, realizing this error before the parent got involved went a long way in avoiding a "you're not fair" battle that I could not feel good about.

Responses to the Fair Word

We'd like to share things that have been effective in deal-ing with parents (or others) when they assert that you have not been fair. Interestingly enough, all of them require you using the F(air) word yourself regularly in response. We will talk about situations as a teacher and as a coach. These approaches can be utilized regardless of our position or responsibilities.

The It-Wouldn't-Be-Fair If-I-Didn't Approach

Let's say that I did attempt to defend my behavior regarding the zero for any missing homework assignment. If I received a call from the parent of that particular student that night—we'll call the student Ricky and the parent Mr. Ricardo—in which the parent brought up the lack of fairness in the way his son was affected, here is how I would respond.

> I appreciate your concern about fair. And what wouldn't be fair, Mr. Ricardo, is if I *didn't* do that. You sound like you are very concerned about *fair* and so am I. And I would not want your son treated unfairly, so in order to treat him *fairly*, I have no other choice. I know that you want Ricky treated the same as the other 120 students I have in my classes so that every-thing is *fair*. And if I didn't give him a zero, it wouldn't be *fair*, so I appreciate your regard for treating your son in the same manner as the other students. So the only way I can be *fair* is to give him a zero. And I value very much your understanding of the importance of being *fair*.

Now, with all approaches in which the educator is the aggressor, there is a fine line between being confident and assertive, and smart aleck and sarcastic. However, having a calm tone and a predetermined dialogue can go a long way toward diminishing the lack of fairness approach. Interest-ingly, we recommend that the more the parents are hung up on this "fair" issue, the more we would use the word fair in our response. If they are very nice and cooperative, we may not even use the word in our reply. However, if they are aggressive parents who center their life on not being treated fairly, then we would sprinkle "fair" very liberally into our response. Again of course, we must always remain calm and work hard to maintain a very confident tone.

The manner and tone we use is essential. Maintaining a confident and professional voice and disposition is critical. As soon as any hint of sarcasm enters your voice, you have just triggered an escalation of this situation, so it is very important that you maintain and monitor the way you deliver your response.

My Daughter's Not Getting Enough Playing Time—It's Not Fair

A situation that every coach has to deal with at some time is a parent saying that their son or daughter is not playing enough on the team. This occurs at every level of sports. Keeping in mind the previous approach, that it wouldn't be fair if I didn't, is the idea that it wouldn't be fair if I did. Here is an example.

Imagine you are a coach of a basketball team and a parent approaches you after practice one day and says, "It's not fair—you do not play my daughter in the varsity games enough!" A potential response that is very effective is to say the following:

> Right now, your daughter is the ninth best player on the team and the fourth best guard. I am playing her about five minutes a game based on her being the ninth best player and the fourth best guard. As you probably know, typically I play our third best guard about 14 minutes a game. However, if your daughter continues to work and practice hard, she may at some point in the future be the third best, second best, or even possibly the best guard on the team. What would not be fair is if at that point she did not get to play as much as the top guards do right now. And I would expect you to be upset with me if she becomes the third best guard on the team and she doesn't get to

play about 14 minutes a game. However, it would not be fair if I did play her more now as fourth best guard because that would limit the time she might receive in the future if she continues to improve.

It is important to help parents and others to understand how being fair now can benefit their son or daughter as the circumstances change. It also allows the parent and student to focus on something—working to improve the student's skills.

Approach Is Everything

Again, the approach you take is essential. Being calm, relaxed, confident, and assertive all at the same time is necessary. Practicing the specific words in the dialogue can allow you to be able to pull them out of your toolkit at the most opportune times. Again, you'll notice in these situations that the more the parents are hung up on the "fair" word, the more it will be in your response. If they are going to try to use it as a weapon, then I am going to pull the "F" word out of my holster in reply. However, you can pair that up with a confident and professional tone that will allow you to make your point in an effective manner.

16

Focus on the Future

Many times when dealing with challenging parents, we have issues that are difficult to agree upon. The version that their child gives could possibly vary "slightly" from the one that we have. Also, the parents may not agree with the consequence that occurs because of their son's or daughter's action. However, finding some common ground that we can agree on is essential. It would be especially valuable if we even have a perspective or point of view that the student, parent, and teacher can all agree on. We can have that perspective by focusing on the future.

Shifting the Conversation

When handling discipline as a teacher or administrator, we find that at times parents may not agree with the consequences that their child has received or may not agree that there should be any punishment at all. Working with these people to develop a common ground and understanding is very critical to being successful and feeling supported as a teacher or school. Additionally, the students may not feel that any punishments they have received are just. However, we can learn that all parties involved can agree on one thing. And that is that they do not

Shifting the focus from the present—which we might not all agree with—to the future can allow for the development of this common understanding.

want it to happen again. Shifting the focus from the present—which we might not all agree with—to the future can allow for the development of this common understanding.

Ask for Their Help

Many of us educators "played school" when we were kids. Dolls, stuffed animals, or even friends or younger brothers and sisters became our "students." We had a chance to practice with them by reading books or explaining things. The stuffed animals were particularly compliant. Seldom did that favorite doll respond by saying, "Make me!" And we certainly never practiced dealing with a phone call when we played imaginary school. Additionally, many of us educators were teacher-pleasers as students, thus we may never have had practice with our families receiving negative calls from school. Thus, when we grow up and become teachers, our experience with that first call home can be very disturbing and rattle our confidence—especially if the parent does not respond in a supportive way. However, if we can move from trying to resolve the point of contention to focusing on the future, we may be able to make even our most dreaded calls more palatable and productive. Whether the issue involves student misbehavior, student unpreparedness for class, or any other repetitive missteps, try centering on prevention versus retribution. Here is an example using something that we likely would never see as a big issue—not bringing a pencil to class. However, I use it because it is one that we will not feel defensive about.

> "Hi, Mrs. Johnson. This is Bill Smith, Amber's English teacher at Eastside High School. I am sorry to bother you at work, but I wondered if I may be able to get your help with something?"
>
> You may think at this point that your most disrespectful parent will just answer an abrupt, "No!" Actually, they are much more likely to wait until they

know what it is before they answer negatively. Please keep in mind that the vast majority of parents will answer, "Yes" or "Of course, what can I do."

You then continue by asking, "Does Amber have any pencils?"

The most negative parents will respond, "Of course she does! We bought her 24 pencils at the start of the year!" Then you would continue in this fashion.

"I asked because she has not brought a pencil three days this week and I do not want her to fall behind in her work nor do I want to get the office involved."

Keep in mind that no parent wants their child to fall behind in their work. And the parents we may be most hesitant to contact often have no faith in authority and they really do not want the office involved! As a result of this approach, you and the parent have come to an agreement and it is really about the future. You are not trying to make them defensive and no one is "in trouble" yet so it is a much easier call when it is about prevention.

Realize that what you are doing is moving away from the past, over which no one has any control, and getting away from the details of this situation (which people may not agree on in some circumstances) to shifting to the future. We would then have the typical discussion asking if Amber had shared this information with them. Then, once again look to the future to conclude the conversation.

Mrs. Johnson, thanks so much for taking the time to chat. I really appreciate you visiting with her tonight because I do not want her to fall behind in her work and I do not want to get the office involved.

A couple of things happened with this approach. We moved from something we (the teacher and the parent) cannot impact—Amber's previous behavior—to something that we all agree on—that we do not want it to happen again. Additionally, if you think back to Chapter 14, on examining the car salesperson, two things the parents remember are that this phone call is a preventative warning and future behavior may affect their child's progress or involve an office referral. And when parents hear the two terms, they realize that the warning sounds like a pretty good deal after all. Additionally, if you do happen to have to contact them again, the parents already know the consequence.

Whether we initiate a parental contact or we receive an unexpected one, being ready to shift to the future can be very beneficial. In the next section, we describe another example of specific language that may help us alter the focus from the present to the future.

What Can We Do to Make Sure This Doesn't Happen Again?

Another way to make the shift to the future is to ask, "What can we do to make sure this doesn't happen again?" Again, we bring a point forward that we can both concur on—that neither of us wants it to happen again. Making sure that we listen, remain calm, and show a genuine interest in a parent's concerns are essential in order to develop credibility and build positive relations. However, it is just as critical that we have specific dialogue that we can rely on in order to help guide difficult conversations to an appropriate and productive conclusion.

If a parent is complaining about grades or a punishment, we may need to center on the past or present, but we should work very hard to move the conversation forward. We can share that we were all disappointed in the grade this quarter, but what can we do to make sure this does not happened again? This allows us to find common ground rather than staying in a place of disagreement. One thing we know about effective student behavior management is that effective people are always looking to prevent misbehavior from occurring again, and less effective behavior managers are looking for revenge for past misbehavior. The basic and most important reason that it is more productive to look to the future is that there is not anything we can do about the behavior that has already occurred. The only thing we can do is to attempt to prevent it from happening again.

Practice Makes Perfect (Or at Least It Makes Better)

Getting all sides to realize the benefit of looking forward to something we can influence is much more empowering then only centering on things that we cannot control. Developing the skills to effectively guide the conversation to the future can be very beneficial. Realize that this skill is appropriate in almost every situation, so we have the opportunity to try it out in more comfortable settings where we are prepared and familiar with the specific language and dialogue. This will allow us to tap into our mental tape recorder and smoothly pull out our focus on the future language during the more stressful and trying settings we may encounter.

Part V

Increasing Parent Involvement

17

Understanding Parent Involvement

Getting and keeping parents involved in our schools is a necessary first step toward developing an understanding of the important role they can play. The more parents are involved in our schools, the more they understand the struggles and challenges that face teachers today. An obvious by-product of this understanding is that these parents become much easier to deal with. They realize that we are all caring, committed educators who want what is best for their children. Even when they question decisions that we may make, they do so in a much more agreeable manner. As an example, consider the comments made by local business or community members after they have visited your school. If you have had the pleasure of involving these individuals in school activities, you have probably heard them make statements such as, "Wow, I never realized just how hard teachers work."

Involving parents at home, as we will elaborate on in Chapter 19, pays similar dividends. When parents are aware of school activities, involved in school governance in some capacity, or helping with their child's homework, then they have a greater understanding

When parents are aware of school activities, involved in school governance in some capacity, or helping with their child's homework, then they have a greater understanding of what takes place at school on a regular basis.

of what takes place at school on a regular basis. Consequently, they become much more understanding and easier to deal with. The important techniques described in previous chapters of this book will not need to be used as often if we are able to make parents less difficult by getting and keeping them involved.

As we mentioned in Chapter 2, parent involvement is unquestionably one of the most significant factors influencing student achievement. Throughout the past few decades, there have been numerous reports and a large body of research stating that parent involvement is a critical factor in the success of students. In fact, to back this research up and to provide guidance for parents and schools, the National Coalition for Parent Involvement in Education (NCPIE) has created a list of goals for improving school-family partnerships.

1. Communication is the foundation of effective partnerships.
2. Schools can reach out through community groups.
3. Families can support schools and children's learning in important ways.
4. Schools should create an environment that welcomes participation.
5. Families model and support children's education at home.
6. Educators can guide families in parent-child activities.
7. Families should be encouraged to develop their own knowledge and skills.
8. Schools can provide cultural education for staff and parents.
9. Leadership training should be provided for educators, staff, and families interested in participating in school governance.
10. Parents are advocates.
11. Schools should collaborate with community organizations.

If parental involvement really is a key to our success as teachers, then is it not time to pay serious attention to it? The 11 goals mentioned by the NCPIE form a good framework.

In further recognition of the benefits of parent involvement in education, some large urban school districts have dramatically increased their focus on this variable in very recent years. The Chicago Public Schools, for example, provide parents with reports that focus on the parents' own role in their children's education. These reports, in the form of checklists, are designed to ascertain the extent to which parents are supporting the school's efforts at home, as well as the parent's success at discharging their own parental duties. Items evaluated include academic ones, such as whether or not students are completing homework assignments and arriving at school with the necessary materials, and parent ones, such as whether or not students are eating breakfast in the morning and arriving at school with the proper medication and clothing appropriate for the weather. They have been utilizing these checklists for almost two decades now. The explosion of social media has made it even easier to regularly put updated versions into the "hands" of parents.

While attention has been increasingly focused on the benefits of parent involvement in schools, the notion of this participation is hardly contemporary. To the contrary, parent involvement in our public schools, both when it was strongly present and noticeably absent, has been a major factor in determining everything from scheduling to curricular choices since before the birth of our country. To understand this and relate it to present parent involvement dilemmas, think about some of the changes parent roles in schooling have undergone. Whereas at one time parents were absent or only in supporting roles relative to their children's schooling, many of them now take on much more decisive roles. This involvement has led to over-involvement in some instances and given rise to such terms as "helicopter parents," those parents who hover constantly over their children's teachers and schools. Consider the summary in the following section as a description of the transitions parent roles have undergone in schooling.

Parents of the Past

Many years ago, near the time of our nation's birth, parents had total control over their children's schooling. Since compulsory attendance laws did not exist, parents had complete authority in deciding how much schooling, if any, their children were to receive. Likewise, because there was far less variety in religious and cultural beliefs than we experience in America today, parents were virtually assured that their values and beliefs would be advanced in school. Additionally, the lack of depth and breadth in curricular choices almost created a guarantee to parents that they themselves would understand what their children learned in school. Parent involvement primarily consisted of reinforcing skills and values that were taught in the schoolhouse. However, the desires of parents with regard to the quantity and quality of schooling their children would receive figured prominently into schoolhouse decisions.

As times progressed, parents saw their roles and the degree of their involvement change a bit. Over time, a new mission for education emerged. Where schools had previously advanced the morals and ethos of families, it quickly became important that they advanced and protected our American culture as well. Parents, though very supportive of the school's goals in creating an educated citizenry, were slowly becoming less involved in the actual structures and designs of these institutions. In their place, famous educators like Noah Webster were making decisions regarding what should be taught and how instruction should be delivered. In advancing his belief that the U.S. should have a uniquely American language, Webster along with William Holmes McGuffy, strongly influenced curriculum during this period. Instead of merely reading the Bible, students were given readers such as the famous *McGuffy Reader*. Parents, valuing the patriotism, heroism, and strong work ethic schools professed, were highly supportive of American schools' endeavors and continued to reinforce their teachings at home. The major curricular decisions, however, were still left to the experts.

As our nation became more global and industrialized, educational theories from other parts of the world quickly infiltrated our American beliefs. The kindergarten movement, born in Germany, is but one example. Additionally, the government became increasingly involved in decisions regarding our schools. Many parents, lacking a strong educational background themselves, began yielding more to the authority of experts regarding what schools should teach and how they should teach it. This is not to say that parents simply gave up all interest in their children's education. To the contrary, many were very involved and supportive. Their involvement had changed, however. Rather than being influential in deciding the content of school curricula, parents were now more involved in supporting the school's decisions. This support manifested itself in fundraising efforts like bake sales and in organized groups, such as PTAs and PTOs. Mothers became the primary supporters of schools while fathers, making up most of the American workforce, took a backseat role.

The preceding paragraphs by no means characterize all aspects of parental roles in American education during a 200-year period. Nor do they acknowledge the differences that existed within and between various American communities. Instead, they merely generalize the role parents played to allow us to better understand the differences between these behaviors and the behaviors of parents today.

Contemporary Parent Involvement

During the second half of the 1900s and continuing today, the role of parents in relation to their children's schools has undergone significant transitions. These transitions have tended to mirror the transitions that have taken place within the larger society. Most notably changed has been the family structure itself. As discussed in Chapter 2, these societal changes have dramatically altered the appearance of the American workforce, thus seriously limiting the time many parents have to be involved in their children's education. Ignoring the fact that schools must change how and when we reach out to contemporary parents and how to involve them in their child's education is to ignore the very nature of these changes.

As mentioned earlier, of equal significance is the fact that many parents of today had very negative experiences in school when they were children. This is truer today than it was when curricular choices were limited, compulsory attendance laws were absent or unenforced, and the requirements put on education by the American workforce were lighter burdens to bear.

Some parents feel intimidated and unwelcome at school. Many parents had negative school experiences themselves or are so unfamiliar with American culture that they do not want to get involved or feel unsure about the value of their contributions. Barriers are also created by parents who have feelings of inadequacy or are suspicious of or angry with the school (Jones, 2001). I know that if my time is limited and I must choose between participating in an activity I enjoy or participating in an activity that intimidates me, my choice becomes rather simple. There are reasons a parent might feel intimidated by a teacher or hesitant to come to the school for a meeting or a conference. Imagine for example, the parent who leaves work and drives 45 minutes during the worst traffic of the day, only to have a brief five-minute conversation with his child's teacher. Parents also become intimidated when they feel a teacher may be questioning their competence as parents, and so when they come for a meeting, they come with a very defensive stance. Parents could be anticipating bad news. They may be surprised if the teacher has something nice to say. Teachers need to work constantly to build parents' confidence that their school encounters will result in positive interactions and success for their child.

After consideration of these points, it is significant to point out some elements of what good parent involvement looks like at the dawn of this new century. According to the National Coalition for Parent Involvement in Education, schools that are successful with parent involvement:

♦ Assess families' needs and interests about ways of working with the schools.

♦ Set clear and measurable objectives based on parent and community input to help foster a sense of cooperation and communication among families, communities, and schools.

♦ Hire and train a parent/family liaison to directly contact parents and coordinate family activities. The liaison should be bilingual as needed and sensitive to the needs of family and the community, including the non-English-speaking community.

♦ Develop multiple outreach mechanisms to inform families, businesses, and the community about family involvement policies and programs through newsletters, slide shows, videotapes, and local newspapers.

♦ Recognize the importance of a community's historic, ethnic, linguistic, or cultural resources in generating interest in family involvement.

♦ Use creative forms of communication between educators and families that are personal, goal oriented, and make optimal use of new communication technologies.

♦ Mobilize parents/families as volunteers in the school assisting with instructional tasks, meal service, and administrative office functions. Family members might also act as invited classroom speakers and volunteer tutors.

♦ Provide staff development for teachers and administrators to enable them to work effectively with families and with each other as partners in the educational process.

♦ Ensure access to information about nutrition, healthcare, services for individuals with disabilities, and support provided by schools or community agencies.

♦ Schedule programs and activities flexibly to reach diverse family groups.

♦ Evaluate the effectiveness of family involvement programs and activities on a regular basis.

As you can see from this list, the role of our schools in relation to family needs has strengthened and increased

dramatically. No longer are schools seen as institutions existing solely for the purpose of imparting knowledge to children.

Modern schools are tasked to meet cultural, social, and educational needs of families . . . This not only requires schools to reach out to parents, but it also encourages them to utilize parents as resources.

Rather, modern schools are tasked
to meet cultural, social, and educational needs of families as well.
This not only requires schools to
reach out to parents, but it also
encourages them to utilize parents as resources. Not doing so
would make the large-scale task
schools face larger and perhaps
insurmountable.

Effectively dealing with our most difficult parents requires
us to understand the importance and nature of their involvement. In the school business, whether we are school leaders,
teachers, or support staff members, we are dealing with people's most precious commodity—their children. Being mindful
of this every time a difficult parent enters our school will help
us to at least understand a small piece of where the parent is
coming from.

18

Increasing Parent Involvement at School

"The most significant type of involvement is what parents do at home. By monitoring, supporting and advocating, parents can be engaged in ways that ensure that their children have every opportunity for success."

(García & Thornton, 2014)

The above quote has always been true, but it leads to an important question. Given what we now know and understand about parental involvement, how do we increase it for the benefit of all of our students? More specifically, what are some methods that schools can use to increase parent involvement and make it productive? These two questions concern teachers all across the country. Regardless of the demographics of any particular school, the notion of parent involvement's value is the same. It doesn't matter if your school is on the East Coast, the West Coast, or someplace in between. Whether your school can be classified as rural, urban, or any place in between is completely irrelevant. Simply put, students are more successful in schools that foster cooperation and personal relationships between school personnel

Students are more successful in schools that foster cooperation and personal relationships between school personnel and parents.

and parents. The kind of parent-teacher collaboration that our students need can't happen without a strong flow of communication. Said another way, "Communication between the home and the school is vital to increasing and sustaining parent-school collaboration" (Waterman, 2006).

The concept of community and the sense of schools as communities can't be overstated. One of the strengths of American public schools has always been the important role that they have played as centers of the community. However, these feelings of community can no longer be taken for granted. Many schools built in the last two decades have been built on parcels of land that are not in neighborhoods. As a result, we have to deliberately build a sense of community, even a virtual one, and affirm its values. The task of making our schools function as communities lies in the hands of teachers. The connections that are built when teachers take deliberate action to transform their schools into communities are strong and necessary.

Allowing parents to believe that they are important members of our school communities is no easy task. Due to lots of issues, many of which we have already discussed, a large percentage of our parents simply don't believe that we deem their involvement to be at all important. Elaine McEwan, educational consultant and author, offers 50 suggestions for getting parent involvement and support started. Included in her list are school climate and school culture issues, such as creating an inviting, welcoming atmosphere and holding regularly scheduled open houses and parent-teacher conferences. These kinds of activities strengthen the feelings of openness and goodwill that are so important. Also, these structured or forced gatherings of parents and teachers together helps to break down the invisible wall that so many parents feel standing between them and the school. However, we submit that they are not enough. There are many other ways, outside of the traditional ones, in which parents and teachers can be partners within the walls of the school.

Think for a moment of your own positive school activities, which have involved parents in significant ways. In all likelihood, you will recall strong feelings of commonality and at least a temporary "breaking down" of barriers between parents and the school. We have both taught in schools that hosted several fun fairs and field day activities that required parents and teachers to work side by side. The equalization of these two distinct roles that came about as a result of these activities was, in all cases, positive. Parents saw teachers in a new light, and teachers saw a very cooperative, caring side of parents. Perhaps more importantly, students enjoyed seeing their parents working with their teachers. This was particularly so when the students liked the teacher in question. As part of our own humanity, we all enjoy introducing people that we respect and admire to one another. We can recall many instances in which a respected colleague, supervisor, or teacher was introduced to one of our family members. It brought us great joy to have these two people, whom we admired and respected, meet each other for the first time. Think, for a moment, about elementary school open houses and parent-teacher conferences. While some students fear what might be said at those conferences, even those kids love the idea that their parents will meet and get to know their teacher, and vice versa.

Obviously, an organization that greatly supports parent involvement in our schools is the National PTA. In addition to writing several position statements and resolutions about school-parent partnerships, the organization has asked that accredited teacher preparation programs in colleges and universities include in their curricula lessons about how to improve these valuable collaborations. In their National Standards for Family-School Partnerships, they offer the following six standards for all teachers and schools to employ in their daily practice:

Standard 1: *Welcoming all families into the school community*—Families are active participants in the life of the school, and feel welcomed, valued, and connected to each other, to school staff, and to what students are learning and doing in class

Standard 2: *Communicating effectively*—Families and school staff engage in regular, two-way, meaningful communication about student learning.

Standard 3: *Supporting student success*—Families and school staff continuously collaborate to support students' learning and healthy development both at home and at school, and have regular opportunities to strengthen their knowledge and skills to do so effectively.

Standard 4: *Speaking up for every child*—Families are empowered to be advocates for their own and other children, to ensure that students are treated fairly and have access to learning opportunities that will support their success.

Standard 5: *Sharing power*—Families and school staff are equal partners in decisions that affect children and families and together inform, influence, and create policies, practices, and programs.

Standard 6: *Collaborating with community*—Families and school staff collaborate with community members to connect students, families, and staff to expanded learning opportunities, community services, and civic participation.

Understanding the reasons for welcoming and involving parents in your school is only half of the battle. The trickier and more sensitive half is figuring out how to actually do it. In your own experiences, you are probably aware of schools that use innovative, purposeful efforts to increase the involvement of all parents. Sharing every conceivable program in this book would be an exhaustive, impossible task. Some of these efforts are unique, serving the special needs of the community in which the school is located. Still others are broader in their appeal. As such, with few modifications, they could be implemented in virtually any school. The list that follows contains some ideas that could really increase parent involvement and support of your school, while also making parents knowledgeable about the learning that takes place at your school. These ideas differ in their magnitude, target audience, and focus. But they all accomplish the goal of involving parents in their children's education at school.

Parent Involvement Can Be Improved and Enhanced by:

♦ Utilizing parent volunteers to assist teachers with office tasks that don't involve the sharing of any student information.

♦ Breaking with tradition by scheduling *at least* two parent-teacher conferences per year.

♦ Purchasing parenting books, magazines, and other materials, advertising your school selection, and giving parents an opportunity to borrow the materials for review.

♦ Creating parent resource centers.

♦ Planning and engaging in other activities determined by the school to be beneficial to promoting and supporting responsible parenting. Bringing in speakers who can talk to parents about parenting.

♦ Scheduling parent volunteers to listen to children read.

♦ Scheduling regular "Parents Make the Difference" evenings where parents are given a report on the state of the school and an overview of:

  ○ What students are learning.

  ○ How students are being assessed.

♦ Starting morning or after-school homework clubs where parents can come and assist students.

♦ Incentivizing a parent involvement night concurrent with a dance or other social event by saying that students get in free with an accompanying parent.

♦ Involving parents in school beautification projects.

♦ Publishing a volunteer resource book, listing the interests and availability of volunteers for teachers' use.

♦ Asking one staff member in your school to serve as a "parent facilitator." This parent facilitator could organize training for teachers and parents that promotes and encourages a welcoming atmosphere to parent involvement in the school.

What these ideas have in common is the understanding that schools need parents to assist in their day-to-day operations. Additionally, many of these ideas include an element of appreciation that is shown to the parents. If we, as teachers, wish to reduce the frequency of our most difficult parent encounters, doesn't it stand to reason that accomplishing this requires us to show our appreciation to helpful parents? We think it does. Our experience as teachers shows us that nothing improves a person's hearing more than praise. Therefore, praise your parents for all of the ways that they assist you. Do so sincerely. You may be surprised at the reduction of difficult encounters you have with parents once you recognize and implement this.

Obstacles to Involving Parents at School

We need to recognize that several structural difficulties exist in some schools that pose additional challenges to keeping parents involved. One simple example is the actual size of the school. Without question, parents of children who attend very large schools often feel more intimidated by the school than do parents of children in smaller schools. There is also a tendency in larger schools for parents to feel as if they get physically lost. But what, if anything, can a teacher do about this? For one thing, anytime you have a parent volunteer scheduled to come to your classroom, you can have a student pick the parent up in the office and escort him or her to the classroom. Not only will this ease the parent's concern about the school size, but it also will make their day when a polite student navigates the maze of the school building with them.

Another obstacle to parent involvement at school is the conflict between the time constraint of a typical school day and the time during which the parent has to work. There are some evening activities at many schools that provide wonderful opportunities to involve parents while avoiding this obstacle, but the majority of school activities do take place at the same exact time as the majority of parents' workdays. In these cases, teachers should give parents opportunities to be involved in school activities from the comfort of their home. Chapter 19 gives advice on how this can be done.

A third, and growing, obstacle is described in the next section. Simply put, it's no longer possible for parents to simply show up at school, walk through the door, and come down to your classroom to help.

Guilty Until Proven Innocent?

Although unintended, we often alienate parents by our safety structures, which effectively make visitors feel unwelcome. Of course, each of us wants and needs our schools to be safe. Equally important, we want our parents to perceive our schools as being the safest possible places for them to send their children. Readers who are parents would agree that school safety is of optimum importance. Announcing your commitment to school safety as soon as a visitor enters the building is, therefore, an excellent idea. How you choose to announce it is another matter altogether, though. Think back to the points in Chapter 7 about the welcoming greeting that meets parents when they arrive at your school's doors. The importance of greeting all visitors with a friendly, welcoming statement really can't be repeated often enough. As teachers who are concerned with cultivating positive relationships with parents, we need to ensure that the guiding message behind all of our interactions with parents is, "We're glad you're here." Anything less than that contributes, though often unintentionally, to the negative feelings that some of our parents have. We are all for increased safety measures designed to keep students secure while they are at school. What we have difficulty understanding is unfriendly methods for employing increased safety. Let's not make parents feel as though they are guilty of wrongdoing the moment they enter our school. Instead, we need to subject parents to whatever level of screening and signing in that is appropriate for our school community in a non-threatening, comfortable, and extremely friendly way.

A related concern involves the use of "badges" or "stickers" that visitors wear when they are in school buildings. In a nutshell, the purpose of these badges is to identify the visitor and/or show individuals who are in regular attendance (i.e., students and staff) that this visitor has, in fact, already reported to the office. We have both been in schools where only some of the visitors were wearing these badges. For the most part, these visitors fell into one of two categories. Either they were (a) individuals who rarely visited the school and would not be recognized by many people, or (b) highly recognized people who habitually follow rules. Other visitors, typically those who were often in the school and were known by virtually everybody, wandered around without picking up a badge in the office. In many cases, rather than risk insulting these people by confronting them, staff members in these schools allowed the visitors to be in the school without badges. This is unfair and upsetting to many parents. Consider the message we are giving visitors when we only require some of them to wear visitors' badges. Though not necessarily intentional, we are saying that highly recognized visitors hold status different from those who only visit us occasionally. Either everybody should wear a visitor's badge or nobody should. Today, with the safety concerns our schools have, the best answer is for everybody to wear them.

As teachers, we need to rethink parent involvement, we need to believe in its importance, and we need to show appreciation to the parents that are involved. We need to be creative in welcoming parents to school, and we must provide opportunities to help them to be involved at school. In doing so however, we can't confuse involvement with support. It's great when we can get both from parents, but we never can confuse the two things. Many parents are supportive of our efforts, but they simply can't be involved. At least, they don't think they can be involved because we haven't helped them to rethink what involvement means. While this chapter has provided some ideas for rethinking involvement at school, as Chapter 19 illustrates, involvement and support from home can sometimes be even more important.

> *We can't confuse involvement with support. It's great when we can get both from parents, but we never can confuse the two things. Many parents are supportive of our efforts, but they simply can't be involved.*

19

Increasing Parent Involvement at Home

In lots of educational literature, parent involvement is defined by parents physically coming to the school building and volunteering. This is largely due to the reluctance of some schools to view parent roles in relation to education differently than they previously had. The apparent unwillingness to acknowledge or embrace change has forced many teachers to view parent involvement from this narrow perspective. Though many aspects of schooling (i.e., technology, assessment, pedagogical knowledge, and scheduling) have undergone admirable changes in recent years, the understanding that parents of today are different from those we may have grown accustomed to has been ignored in many schools. In many schools across the country, parent involvement continues to be reserved for those parents who happen to be available during the regular school day.

It should be obvious to all teachers that schools must consider new ways to get and to keep parents involved. Add to this our knowledge regarding parents' feelings of fear and intimidation at the mere mention of going to their child's school, and it becomes clear that we must discover new and better ways to involve parents from within their own homes. Then, we need to celebrate involvement at

> We need to celebrate involvement at home so that parents know that we appreciate their efforts in reinforcing learning when their children are home and away from school.

157

home so that parents know that we appreciate their efforts in reinforcing learning when their children are home and away from school.

Communication Is the Key

There are numerous ways in which teachers can keep parents involved in their children's education while respecting the fact that many of them are unable or unwilling to physically come to the school. An obvious first step is for the school to regularly communicate with parents. The caveat to remember here is that the best communication is two-way. That is, giving and receiving information are equally important. Some teachers fail in this regard because they mistakenly believe that sending home regular newsletters or email communications and following up on phone calls constitutes effective communication. Though those things are important, they are simply not enough. The best teachers provide opportunities to listen to the concerns of others. From the parents' perspective, these teachers create numerous opportunities for parents to do the talking. They do such things as regularly host social events at school in which parents come to school and collectively speak with them. They place suggestion boxes in accessible places so that parents who are unwilling to initially speak face to face with teachers can still have their concerns heard. They do these things, as well as other innovative things to increase the amount of time spent listening. Fundamental to all human relations or communications training is the concept that people often wish to be heard before they are willing to listen. Teachers, as well as every other school employee, must begin to understand that parents who feel listened to will be much more likely to listen to and trust you.

Teachers, as well as every other school employee, must begin to understand that parents who feel listened to will be much more likely to listen to and trust you.

Though teachers have been hearing about the benefits of regular, purposeful communication with parents for years, it is important for teachers to know that parents are also receiving the same information. The National Coalition for Parent Involvement in Education

(NCPIE), one of the larger and more influential parent advocacy groups, says that schools should regularly communicate with parents about their child's progress and the educational objectives of the school. Furthermore, this organization strongly encourages parents who are not receiving such information to ask for it. Again, the concept of two-way communication is important. This coalition is fulfilling a niche that parents never used to ask for and did not consequently appear to need. Specifically, they are counseling parents about how to get involved in their children's education. In many ways, organizations like this are making the teachers' jobs easier. By offering suggestions to parents, these organizations are informing parents that they need to actively seek involvement in their children's school. Furthermore, they are making the important point that parents can be partners in schooling from within the confines of their own homes. Not only is that a welcome idea for some parents, but also it validates the fact that family needs have certainly changed over time.

This is also a welcome relief to teachers, for it acknowledges that successful parent-school partnerships involve efforts from both parties. It is absolutely true that school personnel must reach out to and involve more parents. It is also true that parents need to take responsibility for having an active role in their children's education, regardless of whether the school appears to be inviting them. This is often where the conflict begins. Parents feel that the school does not welcome them, while the school personnel feel that parents are unwilling to help or be supportive. The bottom line though, a point that has been expanded upon in several previous chapters, is that effective communication is a key in dealing with difficult parents.

Some individual school districts have taken the initiative to inform parents of ways in which they can be involved with school from within their homes. Stephen Kleinsmith, assistant superintendent in Millard, Nebraska, encourages faculty and staff to share the following list of parent involvement options with parents:

◆ Call or email the school staff on a regular basis, and talk with teachers before problems occur.

- Help proofread and edit the school newsletter.

- Become involved in the student's curriculum planning, and discuss academic options with your son or daughter.

- Encourage involvement in the school activities of the student's choice.

- Ask your son or daughter, "What good questions did you ask today?" or "What did you learn in school today?" Then practice good listening, a key to effective communication.

- Encourage reading, using the library, and purchasing books at a young age.

Though not exhaustive, these suggestions can form the foundation of any school's efforts at increasing parent involvement. Essentially, all that is required is for educators to recognize the value of parent involvement in a child's education. Then, educators must communicate to parents that there are ways in which they can be involved without ever having to come to school during regular school hours.

Supporting School from Home

Many successful teachers routinely inform parents of things they can do at home to support their children's learning. Less effective teachers just assume that parents already know how to support their efforts.

Many successful teachers routinely inform parents of things they can do at home to support their children's learning. Less effective teachers just assume that parents already know how to support their efforts. Don't make this mistake. Parents appreciate any advice teachers can give for how to best help their children at home. As long as the information is not presented in a condescending manner, but is offered in the context of how the parents can best assist the teacher's efforts, it is generally well received and considered to be vital information.

What follows are some examples of ideas that parents need to best assist in their child's education from their homes. Parents really can set the stage for learning in everyday activities at home. Here are a few ideas to share with them:

♦ Set a good example by reading.

♦ Read to your children, even after they can read independently. Set aside a family reading time. Take turns reading aloud to each other.

♦ Take your children to the library regularly. Let them see you checking out books for yourself, too.

♦ Build math and reasoning skills together. Have young children help sort laundry, measure ingredients for a recipe, or keep track of rainfall for watering the lawn. Involve teens in researching and planning for a family vacation or a household project, such as planting a garden or repainting a room.

♦ Regulate the amount and content of the television your family watches. Read the weekly TV listing together and plan shows to watch. Monitor the use of DVDs and video game systems.

♦ Ask specific questions about school. Show your children that school is important to you, so that it will be important to them.

♦ Help your children, especially teens manage time. Make a chart showing when chores need to be done and when assignments are due.

♦ Come to an agreement with each of your children on a regular time and place for homework.

♦ Try to schedule homework time for when you or your children's caregiver can supervise.

♦ Make sure your children understand their assignments.

♦ Follow up on assignments by asking to see your children's homework after it has been returned by the teacher. Look at the teacher's comments to see if your children have done the assignment correctly.

♦ Don't do your children's homework. Make sure they understand that homework is their responsibility (www.pta.org/archive_article_details_11180887 22562.html).

In every region of the country, there are lots of success stories about how local schools have developed innovative ways to involve parents who are otherwise unable to come to the school and assist in traditional manners. In addition to the important task of creating positive learning environments at home and speaking positively about school, parents in many school communities are asked to supplement their children's learning at home. The Parent Partnership program in Philadelphia, one innovative example of parent involvement from home, provides reading and mathematics booklets to parents as well as a Dial-A-Teacher assistance project for help with homework in all basic subjects. Many school systems in recent years have expanded on the Dial-A-Teacher concept to include help and assignment information via social media, learning management systems, or email. Also, used in some markets is local access cable television. These telecasts can include advice for parents on providing assistance, as well as the more traditional call-in help programs for students.

The San Diego Unified School District offers materials in both English and Spanish designed to assist in student homework. This is in recognition of the fact that many students do not live in homes that use English as the typical language for communication. As a result, many parents are not involved in their child's school because of an honest barrier to communication. As teachers, we sometimes mistakenly assume that parents have the same command of English as the children we work with do. Often, as the Hispanic population continues to grow throughout the United States, this is not the case. As in San Diego, many school districts are providing information to parents in multiple languages to reduce this obvious barrier to parent involvement.

In addition to assisting schools by supplementing the curriculum, parents are asked to assist in other tasks vital to the success of school programs. At Parkview Elementary School in Valparaiso, Indiana, for example, parents are instrumental in creating the school's annual overnight reading program, Friday Night Live. This program, which temporarily transforms Parkview into a new themed environment each year, is designed to assist children in the association of reading with fun. The school, which has been transformed into an Olympic Village, Hollywood, a beach, a hotel, and a railroad, relies heavily on parent support to accomplish the goals of this program. Though many of Parkview's parents do assist at the school, Friday Night Live requires several months of labor to be completed at home, out of the students' sight. Parents sew, build giant wooden structures, paint, cook, and plan for the event from their homes, during the hours they have available outside of their workdays. Their reward is the delight of students when the big day arrives and the secret theme is revealed. This involvement is as instrumental to student success as involvement that requires parents to be present at school during the academic day. However, it respects the fact that such involvement is not always possible. This, in turn, does a great deal toward strengthening the relationship between parents and school staff at this particular school.

Hopefully you too can think of ways in which your own school utilizes parent volunteers without requiring them to assist at the school during the school day. If not, we encourage you to make the effort to reach out to and involve parents in this way. This will lead to a decrease in the number of difficult parents you encounter, as more of them will begin to recognize their importance on your team. Disagreements with teammates are far less volatile than are disagreements between members of opposing teams. Making parents believe that they are your teammates is

Disagreements with teammates are far less volatile than are disagreements between members of opposing teams. Making parents believe that they are your teammates is an important first step in reducing the number of difficult ones you are required to deal with.

an important first step in reducing the number of difficult ones you are required to deal with.

It's the Simple Things You Do

Keep in mind, though, that parent involvement extends beyond projects that are completed at home. Parents are involved at home every time they take an active role in their child's studies. This key point must be shared with parents on a regular basis. The importance of strong communication skills in dealing with difficult parents has been further elaborated on throughout this book. Informing parents of the importance of reading to their children, monitoring their homework, and discussing expectations regarding conduct and citizenship, all mentioned earlier, are among the most significant ways that schools can involve parents at home. Remember, as we have said, to share this information with parents. Repeat it as many times as is necessary. Again, if I recognize and really believe that you consider me to be important, am I more likely or less likely to be difficult in dealings with you? We think the answer is obvious.

Finally, it is so important to remember that there are specific parenting practices that empirical data has shown are related to students' academic achievement. In fact, according to some researchers and backed up by many teachers, there is an even greater link between student achievement and parent engagement at home than there is between student achievement and parent engagement at school.

Broadly defined, the three types of parent support at home that have most consistently been linked with increased school performance are:

♦ Actively organizing and monitoring the child's time

♦ Helping with homework

♦ Discussing school matters with the child (www2. ed.gov, 2010)

Though the form that these activities take will certainly differ somewhat from family to family, it is vitally important for teachers to consistently affirm their value. We need to stop making parents feel guilty for not being involved with their children at school. At the same time, every one of us needs to inform parents that the activities mentioned in this chapter greatly increase the chances that their children will be successful in school. Parents who recognize this should be celebrated and made to feel like they are valuable members of the school community.

Parting Thoughts

If we've accomplished our goal with this book, you now have some new resources to use with the most challenging of parents or in the most trying of situations. If we always work hard at getting parents on our side, then hopefully we will face fewer challenging people and even soften the difficult situations. But effectively communicating when we do face these tough times is essential. Remember to always be professional and to seem calm yet confident will help stem even the highest of tides.

Even those of us who are already good at connecting with parents need additional items in our bag of tricks that we can rely on in times of need. Hopefully this book has provided some additional tools that all educators can rely on to improve parent relations—which is necessary if we want to educate every student to the best of our ability. Always remember that the more challenging the parents are, the more their child needs us to be the voice of reason and to always model the way a person *should* act rather than reflect the way they *do* act.

Remember that no one likes to deal with these parents (including their own children, unfortunately), but the good people do it anyhow. Teaching is a very demanding profession even in the best of times. It can seem overwhelming if we feel that we are not all pulling in the same direction. Being able to get parents off our backs and onto our sides is a tremendous way to work together for the success of every student.

References

Bissell, B. (1992, July). The paradoxical leader. Paper presented at the Missouri Leadership Academy, Columbia, MO.

Blankenhorn, D. (1995). Pay, papa, pay. *National Review, 47*(6), 34–42.

Brown, J. & Isaacs, D. (1994). *The Fifth Discipline Fieldbook: Strategies and Tools for Building a Learning Organization.* Garden City, NY: Doubleday.

Covey, S. R. (1990). *The Seven Habits of Highly Effective People Restoring the Character Ethic.* New York: Simon & Schuster.

Dietz, M. J. (1997). *School, Family, and Community: Techniques and Models for Successful Collaboration.* Gaithersburg, MD: Aspen Publishers.

Fiore, D. J. (2001). *Creating Connections for Better Schools.* Larchmont, NY: Eye on Education.

Galley, M. (2000). Chicago to size up parents with "checklists." *Education Week, 11*(8), 3.

García, L. E. & Thornton, O. (2014, November 18). The enduring importance of parental involvement. *neaToday.* http://neatoday.org/2014/11/18/the-enduring-importance-of-parental-involvement-2/

Gonzalez-DeHass, A. R., Willems, P. P., & Holbein, M. F. (2005). Examining the relationship between parental involvement and student motivation. *Educational Psychology Review, 17,* 99–123.

Hill, N. E. & Craft, S. A. (2003). Parent-school involvement and school performance: Mediated pathways among socioeconomically comparable African American and Euro-American families. *Journal of Educational Psychology, 96,* 74–83.

Hirshberg, C. (1999, September). How good are our schools? *Life.*

Howard, K. S., Burke Lefever, J. E., Borkowski, J. G., & Whitman, T. L. (2006). Fathers' influence in the lives of children with adolescent mothers. *Journal of Family Psychology, 20,* 468–476.

Jones, D. P. H. (2001). The assessment of parental capacity. In J. Horwath (ed), *The Child's World.* London: Jessica Kingsley.

Lawrence-Lightfoot, S. (1978). *Worlds apart: Relationships between families and schools.* New York: Basic Books.

National Association of Secondary School Principals. (1996). *Breaking Ranks: Changing an American Institution.* Reston, VA: National Association of Secondary School Principals.

National Data Book. (2012). *Statistical Abstract of the United States.* Washington, DC: U.S. G.P.O.

National PTA. (2015). *National Standards for Family-School Partnerships,* pta.org.

National PTA. (2015). www.pta.org/archive_article_details_1118088722562.html

Olsen, G. & Fuller, M. L. (2010). *Home-School Relations: Working Successfully with Parents and Families.* Upper Saddle River, NJ: Pearson.

Phillips, G. (1997, November). Paper presented at the Indiana Principal Leadership Academy, Indianapolis, IN.

Pierce, G. E. (2002). *How Parents Can Save America's Failing Schools.* Philadelphia: Xlbris.

Rank, M. R., Hirschl, T. A. and Foster, K. (2014). *Chasing the American Dream: Understanding What Shapes Our Fortunes.* New York: Oxford University Press.

Schlechty, P. (1997). *Inventing Better Schools: An Action Plan for Educational Reform.* San Francisco, CA: Jossey-Bass.

Sloan, K. (2008). *Holding Schools Accountable: A Handbook for Parents.* Westport, CT: Praeger.

Sterling, M. (1998). Building a community week by week. *Educational Leadership, 56*(1), 65–68.

Strickland, G. (1998). *Bad Teachers: The Essential Guide for Concerned Parents.* New York: Pocket Books.

Tingley, S. Z. (2015). *Smart Parents, Successful Kids: How to Get What Your Child Needs (And Deserves) from Your Local School.* Houseman Press.

Turtel, J. (2005). *Public Schools, Public Menace: How Public Schools Lie to Parents and Betray Our Children.* New York: Liberty Books.

Tyre, P. (2011). *The Good School: How Smart Parents Get Their Kids the Education They Deserve.* New York: St. Martins Griffin.

U.S. Bureau of Labor Statistics. (1987). Online source: http://stats.bls.gov.

U.S. Bureau of Labor Statistics. (2015). Online source: http://stats.bls.gov.

U.S. Census Bureau. (2012). Online source: www.census.gov.

U.S. Conference of Mayors. (1998). Online source: www.usmayors.org.

U.S. Department of Education. (2010). www2.ed.gov. Washington, DC.

Vissing, Yvonne M. (1996). *Out of Sight, Out of Mind: Homeless Children and Families in Small-Town America.* Lexington, KY: University of Kentucky Press.

Waterman, R. (2006). *Breaking Down Barriers, Creating Space: A Guidebook for Increasing Collaboration Between Schools and the Parents of English Language Learners.* Denver, CO: Colorado Department of Education.

Whitaker, T., Zoul, J., & Casas, J. (2015). *What Connected Educators Do Differently.* New York: Routledge.

Yao, E. (1988). Working effectively with asian immigrant parents. *Phi Delta Kappan, 70*(3), 223–225.

9 781138 938670